Be Prepared
for the

AP
Computer
Science
Exam

Maria Litvin

Phillips Academy, Andover, Massachusetts

Practice exam contributors:

H. Donald Allen and Craig Morgan Steele
Troy High School, Fullerton, California

Sally Bellacqua and Mary Dring Johnson
Thomas Jefferson High School for Science and Technology, Alexandria, Virginia

Skylight Publishing
Andover, Massachusetts

Library of Congress Catalog Card Number: 99-095124

ISBN 0-9654853-6-6

Cover design: Marshall Henrichs

Skylight Publishing
9 Bartlet Street, Suite 70
Andover, MA 01810

web: http://www.skylit.com
e-mail: sales@skylit.com
           support@skylit.com

1 2 3 4 5 6 7 8 9 10 ML 03 02 01 00 99

Printed in the United States of America

Contents

About the Authors

Maria Litvin has taught computer science and mathematics at Phillips Academy in Andover, Massachusetts, since 1987. She is an Advanced Placement Computer Science exam reader and, as a consultant for The College Board, provides C++ training for high school computer science teachers. Prior to joining Phillips Academy, Maria taught computer science at Boston University. Maria is co-author of *C++ for You++: An Introduction to Programming and Computer Science*, one of the leading high school textbooks for AP Computer Science courses.

H. Donald Allen has taught computer science at Troy High School in Fullerton, California, since 1993. He serves as an AP Computer Science exam reader and teaches C++ workshops for high school computer science teachers through both The College Board and his school district, where he was recently selected as a mentor teacher in computer science. Don also coaches Troy's Computer Science Team, which has finished second twice and third once in the National Continental Mathematics League Computer Science Contest and has been invited to all-star competitions of the American Computer Science League. Before he began teaching, Don developed flight planning software for military aircraft as a system engineer at Rockwell International.

Sally Bellacqua teaches at Thomas Jefferson High School for Science and Technology in Fairfax County, Virginia, where she is the lead teacher for the school's AP Computer Science program. She runs teacher training workshops and helps develop curriculum in both AP CS and AP Calculus. She co-authored two workbooks of computer science materials, the first in Pascal and the second in C++, used throughout the county's high schools. During the 1998-1999 academic year, Sally and Mary Johnson developed extensive student and teacher materials and led teacher discussion groups to implement the AP CS syllabus in C++. Sally earned her bachelors degree in mathematics from Immaculate Heart College in Los Angeles and her masters in mathematics from the University of Illinois.

Mary Dring Johnson holds degrees from the University of Texas and George Mason University. She taught in Fairfax County, Virginia, schools for 20 years, from 1975 to 1995. Since 1996 Mary has worked as a consultant to the school system, helping to develop a C++ curriculum for intro and AP courses used in the county's 23 high schools. During the 1998-1999 academic year, Mary and Sally Bellacqua co-taught an AP CS teacher discussion and training group to implement the AP curriculum in C++, producing extensive student and teacher materials.

Craig Morgan Steele teaches AP Computer Science and mathematics at Troy High School. He was also a faculty consultant for the 1999 AP Computer Science exam reading. While teaching at Troy, Craig earned his masters degree in Mathematics (Education) from Cal State Fullerton. He holds two bachelors degrees from the University of California at Irvine, a B.S. in Applied Mathematics and a B.S. in Information and Computer Science. Going back even further, during high school (Cypress High School, '88) Craig took the 1986 AP CS test. He received a 5.

Acknowledgments

Gary Litvin helped make this book a reality by working closely with all the authors and editing all the sample questions and practice exams. He contributed ideas and wrote solutions for some free-response questions and created the companion web site for this book.

Our most sincere thanks to David Levine of St. Bonaventure University, NY, to Frances Trees of Westfield High School in Westfield, N.J., and to Dennis McCowan of Weston High School in Weston, Mass. Dave, Fran, and Dennis were very generous in sharing with us their vast experience and first-hand knowledge of the AP CS program and their keen technical insight into computer science and C++. David recommended many important improvements, helped us catch technical mistakes and stylistic blunders, and suggested how we could better balance our practice exams. Fran helped us to streamline our description of The College Board's policies and the AP C++ subset and pointed out several inaccuracies in the technical discussion. Dennis gave us helpful suggestions on how to correct several ambiguities and inaccuracies that he had found in our practice exams.

We are very grateful to Roger Frank of Ponderosa High School in Parker, Colo., who took the time to read a draft very thoroughly, from the introduction to the index, suggested many clarifications of technical points, corrected a number of mistakes, and recommended important stylistic improvements.

We thank Chris Nevison of Colgate University, Chief Faculty Consultant for the AP CS Exams, for taking the time to review a draft of Chapter 1 and making sure our description of the exam requirements and our emphasis of the AP C++ subset and the AP classes is consistent with the intentions of the AP CS program.

Our special thanks to Margaret Litvin for making this book more readable with her thorough and thoughtful editing.

Finally, we thank The Boy Scouts of America for allowing us to allude to their motto in the book's title.

How to Use This Book

Multiple-choice questions in the review chapters are marked by their number in a box:

Their solutions are delimited by ☞ and ☜.

Comments that are relevant only to the AB exam are delimited by ⌈ and ⌋. For example:

> ⌈ The <u>AB exam</u> also includes standard data structures: linked lists, stacks,
> queues, and trees. ⌋

The companion web site

```
http://www.skylit.com/beprepared/
```

is an integral part of the book. It contains the *Case Study* questions, annotated solutions
to free-response questions from last year's exams, and relevant links.

**Be sure to print out the *Case Study* questions from our web site before doing
practice exams.**

Four multiple-choice questions and one free-response question for each exam are on the
web. The answers and solutions to these are on the web, too. The 🖳 icon reminds you to
print them out.

**Our practice exams may be more difficult than the actual exams, so don't panic if
they take more time.**

In the past, A and AB exams shared one or two free-response questions. Our A and AB
practice exams do not overlap but all the questions in our A exams are useful practice for
the AB exam as well. Similarly, the first free-response question in each of our AB exams
(except AB-1, Part (c)) requires only A-level material.

Good luck!

Introduction

The AP exams in computer science test your understanding of basic concepts in computer science as well as your fluency in C++ programming. There are two levels of the exam. The A-level exam covers roughly the material of a one-semester introductory college course in computer science (CS-1). The AB-level exam covers a typical introductory college course plus a second course on data structures (CS-1 + CS-2). Chapter 1 in this book will help you decide which exam you should take.

Exam questions are developed by the AP CS Test Development Committee of The College Board, and exams are put together by the ETS, the same organization that administers SAT, SAT-II and other exams. The College Board offers more than 30 AP exams in 18 subject areas. In 1999 more than a million exams were taken by over 600,000 students. The most up-to-date information on the AP exams can be found on The College Board's web page, http://www.collegeboard.org/ap/.

In the spring of 1999, the computer science exams used C++ for the first time. Planning for the switch from Pascal to C++ started in 1994 and took five years to complete. Developing exams and training exam readers is a very big effort for The College Board; training teachers in a new programming language is another big undertaking. So it is safe to say that C++ will be here to stay for a few years.

Answers to exam questions written in any other programming language will not receive credit.

A working knowledge of C++ is necessary but not sufficient for a good grade on the exam. First and foremost, you must understand the basic concepts of computer science and its common algorithms. ⌈ The AB exam also includes standard data structures: linked lists, stacks, queues, and trees. ⌋

As far as C++ is concerned, you don't have to know the whole language, just the subset defined in The College Board's *Advanced Placement Course Description for Computer Science*. You must also be familiar with The College Board's materials developed specifically for the AP exams: the *AP classes* and the *Case Study*.

This is a lot of ground to cover, and it is certainly not the goal of this book to teach you everything you need to know from scratch. For that you need a complete textbook with exercises and programming projects. (We recommend *C++ for You++: An Introduction to Programming and Computer Science, AP Edition*, and *Workbook to Accompany C++ for You++*, Skylight Publishing, 1998.) Most students who take the exam are enrolled in an AP computer science course at their school. A determined student can prepare for the exam on his own; it may take anywhere between three and twelve months, and a good textbook will be even more important.

The goals of this book are:

- To describe the exam format and requirements
- To describe the AP subset of C++
- To provide a synopsis of the AP classes
- To provide an effective review of what you already know with emphasis on the more difficult topics and on common omissions and mistakes
- To help you identify and fill the gaps in your knowledge
- To provide sample exam questions with answers, hints, and solutions for you to practice on and analyze your mistakes.

The AP exams in computer science are paper-and-pencil affairs. While you need a computer with a C++ compiler to learn how to program and how to implement common algorithms in C++, this book does not require the use of a computer. In fact it is a good idea not to use one when you work on practice questions, so that you can get used to the exam's format and environment. One-hundred-percent correct C++ syntax is not the emphasis here. Small mistakes (a missed semicolon or a brace) that a compiler would normally help you catch might not even affect your exam score. You only need a computer to access our web site for the latest updates and for current materials on the *Case Study*.

Chapter 1 of this book explains the format, required materials, and the C++ subset for the exams and provides information about exam grading and exam-taking hints. Chapter 2 covers the elements of C++ required for the exam. Chapter 3 deals with A exam topics and contains sample multiple-choice questions for each of them with detailed explanations of all the right and wrong answers. Chapter 4 deals with additional AB exam topics. Chapter 5 and Chapter 6 are actually on the web: http://www.skylit.com/beprepared/. Chapter 5 offers annotated solutions to free-response questions from last year's exams. Chapter 6 deals with the *Case Study* (which changes every two to three years). At the end of the book are four complete practice exams — two A and two AB, with no overlap — followed by answers and solutions.

Other subset guidelines:

- Use ++ and -- only on a separate line as shorthand for += 1 (e.g. i++;), and in for loops, but not as terms in larger expressions. For example, a[i++] is strongly discouraged.
- Reference variables may be tested only for passing arguments to functions by reference and by const reference ⌈and, in the AB exam, for returning references from functions ⌋.
- Input and output are limited to cin and cout and text files. Only the >> and << operators and the getline function for the apstring class may be tested. Functions and constructors for opening files, eof() and other stream status checking functions, output formatting and manipulators (except endl), and binary files are not tested.
- Specific constants in limit.h (INT_MAX, INT_MIN), and in float.h and implicit type promotion in arithmetic expressions and especially in function arguments are not tested.

You may find this subset restricting, but showing off on the exam will not earn you any points.

What remains? Actually, quite a bit.

A exam:

- Assignment (=), arithmetic (+, -, *, /, %), increment (++, --), compound assignment (+=, -=, *=, /=, %=), relational (<, >, <=, >=, ==, !=), logical (&&, ||, !), and stream (>>, <<) operators.
- bool, char, int, double data types. enum types. Casts (using function syntax, e.g., double(x)).
- Passing arguments to functions by value, by reference, and by constant reference.
- The apvector and apmatrix classes.
- The apstring class. The getline function.
- Reading from and writing to text files.
- Functions that take istream & and ostream & arguments.
- Structures and classes. Private and public members. Constructors with initializer lists in classes and structures. const member functions. Understanding of (but not necessarily ability to implement) overloaded operators. Understanding of *this.

⌈ <u>AB exam</u>:

All of the above, plus you should be able to:

- Design and implement classes. Implement destructors and copy constructors. Know when to designate a member function `const`.
- Implement templated functions and classes.
- Implement overloaded member and free-standing operators. Use `*this` in member functions.
- Implement nodes in linked lists and trees as structures with pointers. Access structure or class members through pointers using `->`. Allocate and free nodes using the `new` and `delete` operators.
- Use and reimplement the `apstack` and `apqueue` classes. ⌋

This is just the C++ subset outline. The exams include much more material.

1.3. Grading

The exams are graded on a scale from 1 to 5. Grades of 5 and 4 are called "extremely well qualified" and "well-qualified," respectively, and usually will be honored by colleges that give credit or placement for AP exams in computer science. A grade of 3, "qualified," especially on the A exam, may be denied credit or placement at some colleges. Grades of 2, "possibly qualified," and 1, "no recommendation," are basically useless.

Table 1-1 presents published statistics for grades on the 1999 A and AB exams.

Grade	A exam %	AB exam %
5	16.0	31.2
4	24.0	14.6
3	18.6	26.1
2	11.3	10.4
1	30.1	17.7

Table 1-1. 1999 grades distributions for A and AB exams

In 1998, 7,311 candidates nationwide took the A exam and 4,526 candidates took the AB exam; the numbers for 1999 are 12,015 and 6,542, respectively.

The multiple-choice and free-response sections weigh equally in the final grade.

The College Board uses a weighted combination of the multiple-choice and free-response scores to determine the final total score:

```
totalScore = MC_coeff * (countCorrect - .25*countWrong) +
             FR_coeff * FR_score;
```

For multiple-choice questions, as usual, one point is given for each correct answer and 1/4 point is subtracted for each wrong answer. Free-response questions are graded based on a *rubric* established by the chief faculty consultant and a committee of exam readers (high school teachers and college professors). Each free-response question is graded out of 9 points, with partial credit given according to the rubric. The final score is obtained by adding the MC and FR weighted scores. The MC and FR coefficients are chosen in such a way that they give equal weights to the multiple-choice and free-response sections of the exam. For example, if the exam has 40 multiple-choice questions and 4 free-response questions, weights of 1.25 for multiple-choice and 1.3889 for free-response will give each section a maximum total of 50, for a maximum possible total score of 100.

Four cut-off points determine the grade. In 1992, for example, the following cut-off points were used for the AB exam:

Composite score	AP Grade
66 - 100	5
58 - 65	4
40 - 57	3
26 - 39	2
0 - 25	1

On that exam, 66% or more correct would get you a 5. Similar percentages were used for the A exam. The cut-off points are determined by the chief faculty consultant and may vary slightly from year to year, based on the score distributions and close examination of a sample of individual exams.

1.4. A or AB?

Table 1-1 shows that a larger percentage of AB exam takers got a 5. That's how it should be — if you don't feel that you can get a 4 or 5 on the AB exam, you don't need to take it. If you haven't covered all the AB material, or are not comfortable with it, take the A exam. It makes little sense to get a 2 or 1 on the AB exam if you could get a 5 or 4 on the A exam. The practice exams in this book will help you make up your mind.

Published statistical analysis results from the 1992 exam show that 96% of students who got at least 25 out of 40 on the multiple-choice section received a 4 or a 5 for the whole exam (80% received a 5). This may or may not be true for our practice exams. You will know only after the exam!

Most colleges will take into account your AP courses and exam grades in admissions decisions if you take your exams early enough. But acceptance of AP exam results for credit and/or placement varies widely among colleges. In general, the A exam corresponds to a CS-1 course (Introductory Computer Science or Computer Programming I), a one-semester course for computer science majors. The AB exam corresponds to CS-1 + CS-2; that is, the first programming course plus a course on data structures, usually a one-year sequence for computer science majors. Some colleges give one-semester credit for the A exam and two-semester credit for the AB exam, as intended. But other colleges may only give one semester credit, regardless of the exam. They may also base their decision on your grade. For example, you may get a full-year credit only if you got a 5 on the AB exam. Some colleges may not give any credit at all.

The College Board's AP program in computer science is a rigorous and demanding program which is comparable to or exceeds the level of the respective first-year computer science courses at most colleges.

If you plan to major in computer science and your college of choice does not recognize a good grade on the AP exam for credit and/or placement, you should examine the reasons carefully. Decide for yourself whether these reasons are valid or just stem from the bias of that college or its computer science department.

But if the college that you definitely want to attend does not give any admissions preference or additional credit for the AB exam, it may be better to swallow your pride and focus on getting a 5 on the A exam.

To do well on the AB exam, you have to be comfortable enough with C++ classes to write constructors with initializer lists, destructors, member functions, and overloaded operators. You must also know linked lists, binary trees, stacks and queues, priority queues, hashing, and big-O analysis of algorithms.

If you know this material, you shouldn't be afraid of the AB exam. Don't assume that it is "just harder." In fact, the A and AB exams differ not in the depth, but in the breadth of material covered. Nor is it assumed that for the AB exam you must write code better or faster.

The exams share many questions, and, once you learn the data structures part, the AB exam questions are not necessarily harder than the questions on the A exam. The AB exam questions have to be more diverse in order to cover all the material in the same number of questions; this may actually make the exam easier for you if you have studied all the AB material. For example, you may just *love* recursive handling of binary trees, but be prone to mistakes in programs that involve iterations and arrays. The AB exam usually has at least one free-response question on linked lists and one on trees, while the A exam may have a seemingly infinite number of questions on arrays and strings.

1.5. Exam Taking Hints

Some things are obvious:

- If you took the time to read a multiple-choice question and all the answer choices but decided to skip it, take an extra ten seconds and guess. Most likely you have eliminated one or two wrong answers even without noticing.
- If a common paragraph refers to a group of questions and you took the time to read it, try each question in the group.
- Do read the question before jumping to the code included in the question.

But there are other important things to know about answering free-response questions.

Remember that all free-response questions have equal weight. Don't assume that the first question is the easiest and the last is the hardest.

In a nutshell: be neat, straightforward, and professional; keep your exam reader in mind; don't show off.

More specifically:

1. Stay within the AP C++ subset.

2. Remember that the elegance and superior efficiency of your code <u>do not</u> count. More often than not, a brute-force approach is the best. You may waste a lot of time writing tricky, non-standard code and trick yourself in the process or mislead your exam readers who, after all, are only human. No one will test your code on a computer, of course.

3. Remember that Part (b) and Part (c) of the question are graded independently from the previous parts, and may actually be easier: Part (a) may ask you to implement a function and Part (b) may simply ask you to use it.

4. Bits of "good thinking" count. You may not know the whole solution, but if you have read and understood the question, write bits of code that may earn you partial credit points. But don't spend too much time improvising incorrect code.

5. Do not erase or cross out solutions if you have no time to redo them, even if you think they are wrong. You <u>won't be</u> penalized for incorrect code and may get partial credit for it. Exam readers are instructed not to read any code that you intended to remove. But if you wrote two solutions, make sure to cross one out.

6. Glance at function preconditions and postconditions quickly — they usually restate the task in a more formal way and sometimes give hints. Assume that preconditions are satisfied — don't add unnecessary checks to your code.

7. If an algorithm is suggested for a function, don't fight it, just do it!

8. Remember that the exam readers grade a vast number of exams in quick succession during a marathon grading session every June. Write as neatly as possible. Space out your code (don't save paper). Leave spaces around all operators:

   ```
   total += a[i];
   ```

   as opposed to

   ```
   total+=a[i];
   ```

9. Always indent your code properly. This helps you and your exam reader. If you miss a brace but your code is properly indented, the reader (as opposed to a C++ compiler) may accept it as correct. Similarly, if you put each statement on a separate line, a forgotten semicolon may not be held against you.

10. Use meaningful, but not too verbose, names for variables. `count` may be better than `a`; `sum` may be better than `temp`; `row`, `col` may be better than `i`, `j`. But `k` is better than `loopControlVariable`. If the question contains examples of code with names, use the same names when appropriate.

11. Don't bother with comments, they do not count and you will lose valuable time. Occasionally you can put a very brief comment that indicates your intentions for the fragment of code that follows. For example:

```
// Draw left border:
...
...
```

12. Don't worry about #includes — assume that all the necessary header files are included.

13. Use recursion only when appropriate: almost always in functions that deal with binary trees, and only if specifically requested or especially tempting otherwise. Sure, you can write a recursive solution to a simple question, but who wants to read it?

14. Don't try to catch the exam authors on ambiguities: there will be no one to hear your case, and you'll waste your time. Instead try to grasp quickly what was *meant* and write your answer.

2.1. Constants and Variables; Arithmetic, Relational, and Logical Operators

Simple data types included in the subset are `bool`, `char`, `int`, and `double`. `enum` may be tested, too.

It is safer to declare all constants and variables at the top of the function body. Do not declare variables in loops or nested blocks.

For example:

```
int Factorial(int n)                    int Factorial(int n)
// precondition:  n > 1                  // precondition:  n > 1
// postcondition: n! = 1*2*3*...*n       // postcondition: n! = 1*2*3*...*n
//               is returned.            //               is returned.
{                                        {
    int product = 1;                         int i;
                                             int product = 1;

    for ( int  i = 2; i <= n; i++)           for (i = 2; i <= n; i++)
        product *= i;                            product *= i;

    return product;                          return product;
}                                        }
```

It's better not to declare vars in loops

You won't be penalized for declarations inside the code, but the preferred style is to declare all variables above the code. It makes your code easier to read, and may help you avoid mistakes.

1

Which of the following statements is true?

(A)   In C++, data types in declarations of symbolic constants are needed only for documentation purposes.

(B)   When compiled C++ code is running, variables of the `double` data type are represented in memory as strings of decimal digits with a decimal point and an optional sign.

(C)   Its data type determines where a variable is stored in computer memory when the program is running.

(D)   Its data type may determine whether a variable may be passed as a specific argument to a particular function.

(E)   In C++, the data type determines how many bytes are needed to represent a variable in memory regardless of a particular compiler or computer system.

☞   This question gives us a chance to review what we know about data types.

A is false: symbolic constants are not all that different from variables, and if you omit the data type in a declaration of either, it defaults to `int`. For example, in a declaration

```
const pi = 3.14;
```

`pi` becomes an integer and actually gets the value of 3.

B is false, too. While real numbers may be written in programs in decimal notation, a C++ compiler converts them into a special floating-point format that takes a fixed number of bytes and is convenient for computations.

C is false. The data type by itself does not determine where the variable is stored. Its location in memory is determined by where the variable is used and its allocation: whether it is a local or a global variable or a dynamically allocated variable.

E is false, too. Unfortunately, C++ is not totally platform-independent. In 16-bit systems, for example, `int` may take two bytes, while in 32-bit systems it takes four bytes.

D is true. Sometimes an argument of a different type may be promoted to the type expected by the function, (e.g., an `int` can be promoted into `double`) but this is not always the case (e.g., a `double` won't work in place of an `apstring`). The answer is D.

_____ *Arithmetic operators* _____

> The most important thing to remember about arithmetic operators is that the data type of the result, even each intermediate result, is the same as the data type of the operands. In particular, the result of division of one integer by another integer is truncated to an integer.

For example:

```
int n = 3;
int result;

result = n * (n+1) / 2;        // result is 6
result = (n / 2) * (n+1);      // result is 4
result = (1 / 2) * n * (n+1);  // result is 0
```

To avoid truncation you have to watch the data types and sometimes use the cast operator. For example:

```
int a, b;
double ratio;
...
ratio = double(a) / b;
// But not ratio = double(a/b) -- this is a cast applied too late!
```

If at least one of the operands is a `double`, there is no need to cast the other one — it is promoted to a `double` automatically, if necessary. For example:

```
double x;
int factor = 3;
x = 2. / factor;   // Calculated correctly: x = .6666...
```

2

Which of the following expressions does not evaluate to 0.4?

(A) `int(4.5) / double(10);`
(B) `double(4 / 10);`
(C) `4.0 / 10;`
(D) `4 / 10.0;`
(E) `double(4) / double(10);`

☞ In B the cast to `double` is done too late — after the ratio is truncated to 0 — so it evaluates to 0. The answer is B. ☜

In the real world we have to worry about the range of values for different data types. For example, the `Factorial` function (p. 13) may overflow the result, even for relatively small *n*.

For the AP exam, you have to be aware of what overflow is but you don't have to worry about the specific limits.

_____ *Modulo division* _____

The % (modulo division) operator applies only to integers: it calculates the remainder when the first operand is divided by the second.

For example:

```
int r;
r = 17 % 3;   // The value of r is 2
r = 8 % 2;    // The value of r is 0
```

_____ ++ *and* -- _____

There are two forms of the ++ and -- operators in C++: the prefix form increments (or decrements) the variable before its value is used in the rest of the expression; the postfix form increments (or decrements) it afterwards.

The Exam Committee discourages the use of ++ or -- in expressions. Use ++ and -- only in separate statements and always use their postfix form.

For example:

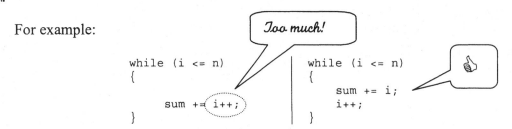

```
while (i <= n)          while (i <= n)
{                       {
                            sum += i;
    sum += i++;             i++;
}                       }
```

You won't lose points over ++ or -- in expressions if you use them correctly, but they won't earn you any credit either!

It is bad style <u>not</u> to use increment or compound assignment operators where appropriate:

```
for (i = 0; i < n; i = i + 1)          for (i = 0; i < n; i++)
{                                      {
    count = count + 1;                     count++;
    sum = sum + a[i];                      sum += a[i];
}                                      }
```

Works, but is this C++?

Again, no penalty but looks ugly.

Arithmetic expressions are too easy to be tested alone. You may encounter them in questions that combine them with logic, iterations, recursion, etc.

_____ *Relational and logical operators* _____

In the subset, the relational operators ==, !=, <, >, <=, >=, will apply to integers, `doubles`, or `apstrings`. Remember that "is equal to" is represented by == (not to be confused with the assignment operator, =). Write it clearly. `a != b` is equivalent to `!(a == b)`, but `!=` is stylistically better.

The logical operators &&, ||, and ! normally apply to Boolean values and expressions. For example:

```
bool found = false;
...
while (i < 0 && !found)
    ...
```

Do not write

```
while (... && !found == true)
```

— this works, but is redundant. Also, note that it's perfectly fine to write `!found` in place of `found == false`.

3

Assuming that x, y, and z are integer variables, which of the following three logical expressions are equivalent to each other, that is, have the same values for any values of x, y, and z?

```
I.    (x == y && x != z) || (x != y && x == z);
II.   (x == y || x == z) && (x != y || x != z);
III.  (x == y) != (x == z);
```

(A)   I and II only
(B)   II and III only
(C)   I and III only
(D)   I, II, and III
(E)   None of the three

☞ Expression III is the key to the answer: all three expressions state the fact that exactly one out of two equalities, x == y and x == z, is true. Expression I states that either the first and not the second or the second and not the first is true. Expression II states that one of the two is true and one of the two is false. Expression III simply states that they have different values. All three boil down to the same thing. The answer is D. ☜

In C++ an integer can be used as a Boolean expression: any non-zero value is interpreted as true, while zero is interpreted as false. You can write, for example,

```
while (n) ...
```

This is the same as:

```
while (n != 0) ...
```

However, the latter form is preferred in AP exams.

⌈ The same applies to pointers when handling linked lists or trees:

```
if (p != NULL)
```

is preferable to

```
if (p) ...
```
⌋

De Morgan's Laws

The exam may include questions on De Morgan's Laws:

```
!(a && b)  is the same as  !a || !b
!(a || b)  is the same as  !a && !b
```

4

The expression `!((x <= y) && (y > 5))` is equivalent to which of the following?

(A)   `(x <= y) && (y > 5)`
(B)   `(x <= y) || (y > 5)`
(C)   `(x >= y) || (y < 5)`
(D)   `(x > y) || (y <= 5)`
(E)   `(x > y) && (y <= 5)`

  The given expression is pretty long, so if you try to plug in specific numbers you may lose a lot of time. Use De Morgan's Laws instead:

$$! ((x <= y) \quad \&\& \quad (y > 5))$$

$$!(x <= y) \quad \boxed{||} \quad !(y > 5)$$

$$(x > y) \quad || \quad (y <= 5)$$

> When ! is distributed, && changes into ||, and vice-versa

The answer is D.

Short-Circuit Evaluation

> An important thing to remember about the C++ logical operators, && and ||, is *short-circuit evaluation*. If the value of the first operand unambiguously defines the result, then the second operand is **not** evaluated.

5

Consider the following code segment:

```
int x = 0, y = 3;
char op = '/';

if ((op == '/') && (x != 0) && (y/x > 2))
    cout << "ok" << endl;
else
    cout << "failed" << endl;
```

Which of the following statements about this code is true?

(A)   There will be a compile error because `char` and `int` variables are intermixed in the same condition.

(B)   There will be a run-time divide-by-zero error.

(C)   The code will compile and execute without error; the output will be `ok`.

(D)   The code will compile and execute without error; the output will be `failed`.

(E)   The code will compile and execute without error; there will be no output.

☞ A and E are just filler answers. Since x is equal to 0, the condition cannot be true, so C should be rejected, too. The question remains whether it bombs or executes. Similar code in Pascal would bomb because there is no short-circuit evaluation there; but in C++ there is, so once `x != 0` fails, the rest of the condition, `y/x > 2`, won't be evaluated, so `y/x` won't be computed. The answer is D. ☜

In the above question relational expressions are parenthesized. This is not necessary because they always take precedence over logical expressions. If you are used to lots of parentheses, use them, but you can skip them as well. For example, the Boolean expression from Question 5 can be written with fewer parentheses:

```
if (op == '/' && x != 0 && y/x > 2) ...
```

&& also takes precedence over ||, but it's clearer to use parentheses when && and || appear in the same expression. For example:

```
if ((0 < a && a < top) || (0 < b && b < top)) ...
```

2.2. `if-else` Statements, `switch`, and Loops

You can use simplified indentation for `if-else-if` statements.

For example:

```
if (score >= 92)
    grade = 'A';
else if (score >= 85)
    grade = 'B';
...
else
    grade = 'F';
```

But don't forget braces and proper indentation for nested `if`s. For example:

```
if (A_Exam)
{
    if (score >= 57)
        grade = 'A';
    else
        ...
}
else    // AB_Exam
{
    if (score >= 66)
        grade = 'A';
    else
        ...
}
```

6

Consider the following code segment, where x is a variable of the type `double`:

```
if (x > 0.001)
{
    if (int(1.0 / x) % 2 == 0)
        cout << "even" << endl;
    else
        cout << "odd" << endl;
}
else
    cout << "small" << endl;
```

Which of the following code segments are equivalent to the one above (that is, produce the same output as the one above regardless of the value of x)?

I.
```
if (x <= 0.001)
    cout << "small" << endl;
else if (int(1.0 / x) % 2 == 0)
    cout << "even" << endl;
else
    cout << "odd" << endl;
```

II.
```
if (x > 0.001 && int(1.0 / x) % 2 == 0)
    cout << "even" << endl;
else if (x <= 0.001)
    cout << "small" << endl;
else
    cout << "odd" << endl;
```

III.
```
if (int(1.0 / x) % 2 == 0)
{
    if (x <= 0.001)
        cout << "small" << endl;
    else
        cout << "even" << endl;
}
else
{
    if (x <= 0.001)
        cout << "small" << endl;
    else
        cout << "odd" << endl;
}
```

(A)   I only
(B)   II only
(C)   I and II
(D)   II and III
(E)   I, II, and III

☞ Segment I can actually be reformatted as:

```
if (x <= 0.001)
    cout << "small" << endl;
else
{
    if (int(1.0 / x) % 2 == 0)
        cout << "even" << endl;
    else
        cout << "odd" << endl;
}
```

So it's the same as the given segment with the condition negated and `if` and `else` swapped. Segment II restructures the sequence, but gives the same result. To see this we can try different combinations of true/false for `x <= 0.001` and `int(1.0 / x) % 2 == 0`. Segment III would work, too, but it has a catch: it bombs when x is equal to 0. The answer is C. ☚

Switch

The `switch` statement has the general form:

```
switch (expression)
{
  case value1:
    ...            // Do something
    break;

  case value2:
    ...            // Do something else
    break;
  ...

  default:
    ...            // Default action
    break;
}
```

It is equivalent to:

```
if (expression == value1)
{
    ...            // Do something
}
else if (expression == value2)
{
    ...            // Do something else
}
...

else
{
    ...            // Default action
}
```

Loops: for, while, and do-while

The `for` loop,

```
for (initialize; condition; increment)
{
    ...    // Do something
}
```

is equivalent to the `while` loop:

```
initialize;
while (condition)
{
    ...    // Do something
    increment;
}
```

increment can mean any change in the values of the variables that control the loop; actually it can be a *decrement*.

`for` loops are shorter and more idiomatic in some instances. They shouldn't be discriminated against. For example:

```
i = 0;
while (i < a.length())
{
    sum += a[i];
    i++;
}
```

Ok

```
for (i = 0; i < a.length(); i++)
    sum += a[i];
```

More idiomatic

The `do-while` loop has the form

```
initialize;
do
{
    ...                    // Do something
    < increment or modify loop control variable(s) >;
    ...
} while (condition);
```

In a `while` loop, the condition is evaluated at the beginning of the loop and the program does not go inside the loop if the condition is false. Thus, the body of a `while` loop may be skipped entirely if the condition is false at the very beginning. A `do-while` loop is different: the program always enters a `do-while` loop since the condition is evaluated at the end of `do-while`.

7

Consider the following functions:

```
int Fun1(int n)                int Fun2(int n)
{                              {
    int product = 1;               int product = 1;
    int k;                         int k = 1;
    for (k = 1; k <= n; k++)       while (k <= n)
    {                              {
        product *= k;                  product *= k;
    }                                  k++;
    return product;                }
}                                  return product;
                               }
```

For which integer values of n do `Fun1(n)` and `Fun2(n)` return the same result?

(A)   Any n > 1
(B)   Any n < 1
(C)   Only n == 1
(D)   Any n >= 1
(E)   Any integer n

☞ The best approach here is purely formal: since the initialization, condition, and increment in the `for` loop in `Fun1` are the same as the ones used with the `while` loop in `Fun2`, the two functions are equivalent. The answer is E. ↵

8

Consider the following two code segments:

```
while (x > y)                      do
{                                 {
    x--;                              x--;
    y++;                              y++;
}                                 } while (x > y);
cout << "x - y = " << (x - y);    cout << "x - y = " << (x - y);
```

Assume that x and y are initialized int variables. Under which of the following conditions will the output of the two code segments be the same?

    I.   x is equal to y just before the code runs.
   II.   x is greater than y just before the code runs.
  III.   x is less than y just before the code runs.

(A)   I only
(B)   II only
(C)   III only
(D)   I and II
(E)   I and III

☞ This exercise tests your understanding of while vs. do-while loops. Since the initial settings, the terminating conditions, and the bodies of the loops are the same, the only possible difference may be in the first iteration. The do-while loop will always run through the first iteration, whereas the while loop will be skipped altogether when the condition is false at the outset. That happens when x <= y. The output is the same when x > y. Note that both loops always terminate. Each iteration decreases the difference between x and y by 2 until it becomes negative. The answer is B. ☜

 *OBOBs*

When coding loops, beware of the so-called "off-by-one" bugs ("OBOBs"). These are mistakes of running through one iteration too many or one iteration too few.

9

Assume the following definitions have been made.

```
bool IsPrime(int p);
// precondition:  p >= 2
// postcondition: Returns true if p is a prime number, false otherwise.

int n = 101;
int sum = 0;
```

Which of the following code segments correctly computes the sum of all prime numbers from 2 to 101?

(A)
```
while (n != 2)
{
    n--;
    if (IsPrime(n)) sum += n;
}
```

(B)
```
while (n >= 2)
{
    n--;
    if (IsPrime(n)) sum += n;
}
```

(C)
```
while (n != 2)
{
    if (IsPrime(n)) sum += n;
    n--;
}
```

(D)
```
while (n >= 2)
{
    if (IsPrime(n)) sum += n;
    n--;
}
```

(E)
```
while (n >= 2 && IsPrime(n))
{
    sum += n;
    n--;
}
```

☞ It is bad style to start the body of a loop with a decrement, so choices A and B are most likely wrong. Indeed, both A and B miss 101 (which happens to be a prime) because n is decremented too early. In addition, B eventually calls IsPrime(1) violating its precondition. C misses 2 — OBOB on the other end. E might look plausible for a moment, but it actually quits as soon at it encounters the first non-prime number. The answer is D. ☜

break and return in loops

It is okay in C++ to use break and return inside loops. return immediately quits the function from any place inside or outside a loop. This may be a convenient shortcut, especially when you have to write nested loops and you are pressed for time. For example:

```cpp
bool AllPositive(const apmatrix<int> & m)
// precondition:   ...
// postcondition: Returns true if all values in the matrix are positive,
//                false otherwise.
{
    int row, col;

    for (row = 0; row < m.numrows(); row++)
        for (col = 0; col < m.numcols(); col++)
            if (m[row][col] <= 0)
                return false;
    return true;
}
```

You can also use break, but remember that in a nested loop break takes you out of the inner loop but not out of the outer loop. Avoid redundant, verbose, and incorrect code like this:

```cpp
bool AllPositive(const apmatrix<int> & m)
// precondition:   ...
// Postcondition: Returns true if all values in the matrix are positive,
//                false otherwise.
{
    int row, col;
    bool foundNegatives;

    for (row = 0; row < m.numrows(); row++)
    {
        for (col = 0; col < m.numcols(); col++)
        {
            if (m[row][col] <= 0)
            {
                foundNegatives = true;
                break;
            }
            else
            {
                foundNegatives = false;
            }
        }
    }
    if (foundNegatives == true)
        return false;
    else
        return true;
}
```

Out of the inner for *but still in the outer* for.

If you insist on using Boolean flags, you need to be extra careful:

```
bool AllPositive(const apmatrix<int> & m)
// precondition:  ...
// postcondition: Returns true if all values in the matrix are positive,
//                false otherwise.
{
    int row, col;
    bool foundNegatives = false;

    for (row = 0; row < m.numrows() && !foundNegatives; row++)
    {
        for (col = 0; col < m.numcols(); col++)
        {
            if (m[row][col] <= 0)
            {
                foundNegatives = true;
                break;
            }
        }
    }
    return !foundNegatives;
}
```

The `continue` statement is not in the AP subset and therefore should be avoided.

2.3. Functions

In C++, a function takes a specific number of arguments of specific data types. Some functions take no arguments. A function call may pass a whole expression as an argument to that function; the expression may include calls to other functions. For example:

```
double x, y;
...
x = sqrt(fabs(2*y - 1));
```

A function usually returns a value of the specified data type, but a `void` function does not return any value. The return value is specified in the `return` statement.

It is regarded a "major error" to read inside a function the new values for its arguments from `cin` or to print inside the function the return value to `cout`.

For example:

```
int AddNumbers (int n)
// precondition:  n >= 1
// postcondition: Returns the sum of all integers from 1 to n.
{
    int k;
    int sum = 0;
```

Mistake 👎

```
    cin >> n;      // n is passed to this function from main or
                   //    from another calling function

    for (k = 1; k <= n; k++)
    {
```

Mistake 👎

```
        sum += k;
    }

    cout << sum;  // Not intended and not described in the postcondition

    return sum;
}
```

10

Suppose the function

```
int Min(int a, int b);
```

returns the value of the smaller of two integers. If a, b, c, and m are integer variables, which of the following best describes the behavior of a program with the following statement?

```
m = Min(Min(a, c), Min(b, c));
```

(A)   The program has a syntax error and will not compile.
(B)   The program will run but go into an infinite loop.
(C)   Both a and b will get the smallest of the values a and b, and m will get the value of c.
(D)   m will be assigned the smallest of the values a, b, and c.
(E)   None of the above

☞ Any expression of the appropriate data type, including function calls that return values of the appropriate data type, may be an argument to a function. The code above is basically equivalent to:

```
int temp1 = Min(a, c);
int temp2 = Min(b, c);
m = Min(temp1, temp2);
```

So m gets the smallest of the three values. The answer is D. ↵

_____ *Arguments passed by value and by reference* _____

You have to recognize when function arguments are passed by value and when by reference and the implications of each. You also have to understand aliasing.

> **When an argument is passed by value, the function works with a copy of the variable passed to it, so it has no way of changing the value of the original. When an argument is passed by reference, the function gets the address of the variable and works with the original. Passing by reference is designated by the & symbol in front of the argument.**

11

Consider the following function:

```
void Fun(int a, int & b)
{
    a += b;
    b += a;
}
```

What is the output from the following code?

```
int x = 3, y = 5;
Fun(x, y);
cout << x << ' ' << y << endl;
```

(A)   3   5
(B)   3   8
(C)   3   13
(D)   8   8
(E)   8   13

☞ The first argument in Fun is passed by value, the second by reference. So the function works with a copy of x and the original y. What is really happening here might be represented like this:

```
int x = 3, y = 5;

int x2 = x;          // x2 becomes 3
x2 += y;             // x2 becomes 8
y += x2;             // y becomes 13

cout << x << ' ' << y << endl;
```

So x doesn't change after the function call. This eliminates choices D and E. y can and does change: x2 gets the value of 8, then y gets the value of 13. The answer is C. ↵

_____ *Passing by const reference* _____

Often we want to pass an argument by reference not because the function changes it, but because, for the sake of efficiency, we want to avoid copying the value. This usually applies to arrays, strings, and structures. We use a `const` reference argument when the function does not change it to enforce and document that fact.

For example:

```
int CountConsonants(const apstring & name);
bool AllPositive(const apmatrix<int> & m);
```

_____ *Aliasing* _____

A more complicated concept is aliasing. Consider a function:

```
void Move2 (const apvector<int> & a, const apvector<int> & b,
                             apvector<int> & c, apvector<int> & d)
// postcondition:  a is copied into c; b is copied into d.
{
    c = a;
    d = b;
}
```

In this example we work with `apvector` arguments because it makes sense to pass them by reference. The code looks pretty harmless: it moves a into c and b into d. Now suppose you call `Move2 (x,y,y,x)`, hoping to swap the vectors x and y. The compiler will not prevent you from doing that, but the result will not be what you expected. Then, inside the function, a and d actually both refer to x, and b and c both refer to y. The first statement, `c = a`, will set y equal to x, and the value of y will be lost. Instead of being swapped, both arguments will be set to x. This type of error is called aliasing error.

Aliasing may happen when arguments are passed by reference ⌈ or when arguments are pointers, or when arguments are classes or structures that contain pointers... ⌋.

If you want this function to work for any arguments, including the aliasing case, you have to change the code:

```
void Move2(const apvector<int> & a, const apvector<int> & b,
                            apvector<int> & c, apvector<int> & d)
{
    apvector<int> tempA = a;
    apvector<int> tempB = b;
    c = tempA;
    d = tempB;
}
```

Seems redundant, but it's "aliasing-proof."

12

Consider the following function:

```
int Stretch (int & x, int & y)
{
    x *= 2;
    y *= 2;
    return x * y;
}
```

What is the output from the following code?

```
int q = 3;

cout << Stretch(q, q) << ' ';
cout << q << endl;
```

(A)   9 3
(B)   18 3
(C)   36 6
(D)   36 12
(E)   144 12

☞ This is a very artificial question: the function is a bit of a stretch. But it is a simple way to illustrate aliasing. Note that x and y are passed to Stretch by reference. Normally, if x and y were different variables, Stretch would double each of them, then return the product of their new values, that is, four times the product of their original values. So potentially we could expect the output to be 36 6. But here we call Stretch with the same variable for x and y: both x and y refer to q. So the code in Stretch first doubles q, then doubles it again, then returns the new value squared.

In other words, here is what happens:

```
                        // q = 3; x and y refer to q
x *= 2;                 // q = 6
y *= 2;                 // q = 12
return x * y;           // q = 12; returns 12 * 12 = 144
```

The answer is E.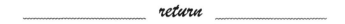

------------------------------- *return* -------------------------------

A function other than `void` must return a value of the designated type using the `return` statement. `return` works with any expression, not just a variable. For example:

```
return (a + sqrt(b*b - 4*a*c)) / (2*a);
```

An often overlooked fact is that a `bool` function can return the value of a Boolean expression. For example, you can write simply

```
return x >= a && x <= b;
```

as opposed to the redundant and more verbose

```
if (x >= a && x <= b)
    return true;
else
    return false;
```

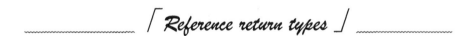
--------------- ⌈ *Reference return types* ⌋ ---------------

⌈ AB students should be able to "read and use reference return types." The reference return is usually encountered in overloaded operators. For example:

```
istream & operator >> (istream & is, ...);
```

This operator returns a reference of the type `istream`. In this case it simply returns back the first argument, `is`. This is a convention for overloading stream input and output operators.

You should understand "the implications of returning reference to a local variable." A reference represents an address, and it makes little sense to return the address of a local variable from a function because all local variables disappear (are no longer allocated) after the function is exited. So the implication of returning and using a reference to a local variable is that your program crashes. You can return it safely, of course — as long as you never use it. ⌋

2.4. Arrays, the `apvector` and `apmatrix` Classes

In all AP materials, one- and two-dimensional arrays are represented by the `apvector` and `apmatrix` classes, respectively.

There are three ways to declare a one-dimensional array of, say, integers:

```
apvector<int> v;          // length 0
apvector<int> v(10);      // length 10
apvector<int> v(10, 99);  // length 10; all values set to 99
```

The first declaration declares an empty array of length 0. It has to be resized before it can be used. The second and third declarations declare an array of size 10; in addition the third declaration sets the values of all its elements to 99. You can use any valid constants, variables, or expressions instead of 10 and 99. For example:

```
const int size = 50;
apvector<int> grades(size);
```

An array of `bool`, `char`, `double`, or strings is declared in a similar way. For example:

```
apvector<bool> answers(40, true);
apvector<double> sample(100);
apvector<char> stars(5, '*');
apvector<apstring> cities(10, "");   // All values set to empty string
```

Consider the following function:

```
void Add(const apvector<double> & x, const apvector<double> & y,
                                     apvector<double> & z)

// precondition:  apvectors x and y have the same size and are filled
//                with values.
// postcondition: z is set to the same size as x and y.
//                z[k] = x[k] + y[k]; 0 <= k < x.length()
{
    int k;
    int len = x.length();

    z.resize(len);

    for (k = 0; k < len; k++)
    {
        z[k] = x[k] + y[k];
    }
}
```

The above code uses almost everything there is to know about the `apvector` class:

- `apvector` arguments should be always passed to functions by reference, or by constant reference if that argument is not changed in the function.
- The `length()` member function returns the size (the number of elements) of the vector.
- The `resize(int newSize)` member function sets the size of the vector to a given non-negative number. It is important to make sure that the size is set before you use the vector.
- You can access individual elements of an `apvector` using subscripts, in the same way as for standard arrays. Subscripts start from 0. An element with a subscript may be either an *rvalue* or an *lvalue*, that is, it may appear either on the right- or left-hand side of the assignment operator.

The apvector class checks that a subscript's value falls into the legal range — from 0 to `length()-1` — and if it doesn't, the class generates a run-time (not a compile-time) error and terminates the program.

One other thing to know is the assignment operator for `apvector`. Given `apvectors` `v1` and `v2` whose elements are of the same data type, you can write simply:

```
v2 = v1;
```

instead of copying them element by element. The assignment operator adjusts the size of `v2`, if necessary, and then copies each element of `v1` into the corresponding location in `v2`.

13

The function `int sign(int x)` returns 1 if x is positive, -1 if x is negative, and 0 if x is 0. If the values of the first five elements in an array A are -2, -1, 0, 1, 2, what are the values of these elements after the following code is executed?

```
int k;
for (k = 0; k < 5; k++)
{
    A[k] -= sign(A[k]);
    A[k] += sign(A[k]);
}
```

(A) -2, -1, 0, 1, 2
(B) -1, 0, 0, 0, 1
(C) 0, 0, 0, 0, 0
(D) -2, 0, 0, 2, 3
(E) -2, 0, 0, 0, 2

☞ Remember that the first statement within the loop changes A[k], which may change the sign of A[k], too. Jot down a little table:

Before		After -=		After +=
a[k]	sign of a[k]	a[k]	sign of a[k]	a[k]
-2	-1	-1	-1	-2
-1	-1	0	0	0
0	0	0	0	0
1	1	0	0	0
2	1	1	1	2

The answer is E. ↵

14

Consider the following function:

```
bool Sparse(const apvector<int> & A, int n)
// precondition:  A contains n values, n > 1.  Values are stored
//                in positions 0 to n-1 in any random order.
// postcondition: Returns true if there are no two elements in A
//                whose values are the same or are consecutive
//                integers.
{
    int j, k, diff;

    < code >
}
```

Which of the following code segments can be used to replace < *code* > so that function Sparse satisfies its postcondition?

I.
```
for (j = 0; j < n; j++)
{
    for (k = j + 1; k < n; k++)
    {
        diff = A[j] - A[k];
        if (diff >= -1 && diff <= 1)
            return false;
    }
}
return true;
```

II.
```
for (j = 1; j < n; j++)
{
    for (k = 0; k < j; k++)
    {
        diff = A[j] - A[k];
        if (diff >= -1 && diff <= 1)
            return false;
    }
}
return true;
```

III.
```
for (j = 0; j < n; j++)
{
    for (k = 1; k < n; k++)
    {
        diff = A[j] - A[k];
        if (diff >= -1 && diff <= 1)
            return false;
    }
}
return true;
```

(A)   I only
(B)   II only
(C)   I and II only
(D)   I and III only
(E)   I, II, and III

☞ Note that in this question not all `A.length()` elements of `A` are used, just the first *n*. Their subscripts range from 0 to *n*-1. The precondition states that $n > 1$, so there is no need to worry about an empty array or an array of just one element. Looking at the inner loop in each segment you can quickly see that they are the same. So the difference is in how the loops are set up; more precisely, in the limits in which the subscripts vary. In Segment I the outer loop starts with the first element in the list; the inner loop compares it with each of the subsequent elements. In Segment II the outer loop starts with the second element in the list; the inner loop compares it with each of the previous elements. Both of these are correct and quite standard in similar algorithms. This eliminates A, B, and D. Segment III at first seems harmless, too, but it has a catch: the inner loop doesn't set a limit for `k` that depends on `j`, so when `j` is greater than 0, `k` may eventually take the same value as `j`, (e.g. `j` = 1, `k` = 1). The function will erroneously detect the same value in `A` when it is actually comparing an element to itself. The answer is C. ⇗

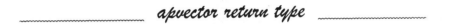

apvector return type

Occasionally you may need to return a vector from a function. Suppose you want to restructure the `Add` function above so that it <u>returns</u> a new vector equal to the sum of the two operands. Then it can be coded as follows:

```
apvector<double> Add(const apvector<double> & x, const apvector<double> & y)
// precondition:  apvectors x and y have the same size and are filled
//                with values.
// postcondition: Returns a new array z of the same size as x and y
//                with z[k] = x[k] + y[k], for 0 <= k < x.length()

{
    int k;
    int len = x.length();
    apvector<double> z(len);

    for (k = 0; k < len; k++)
        z[k] = x[k] + y[k];

    return z;
}
```

———————————— *apmatrix* ————————————

The `apmatrix` class is similar to the `apvector` class, but an `apmatrix` may be declared with two arguments, the number of rows and the number of columns, instead of one, size. The following are examples of valid declarations of two-dimensional arrays:

```
apmatrix<double> radiationLevels;      // Declares an empty matrix
                                       //    (with 0 rows and 0 cols)
apmatrix<bool> reservedSeats(10, 30);  // A matrix with 10 rows and 30 cols
apmatrix<char> stars(50, 10, '*');     // A matrix with 50 rows and 10 cols
                                       //    with all elements set to '*'
```

The `apmatrix` class has two member functions, `numrows()` and `numcols()`, in place of `length()`. The `resize()` function takes two arguments, the number of rows and the number of columns.

Consider the following function that calculates the sums of elements in each column of a matrix:

```
void TotalByColumns(const apmatrix<double> & table, apvector<double> & total)

// precondition:   table is a 2-D array with the dimensions
//                 numcols() by numrows().
// postcondition:  total[c] is set to the sum of all the elements
//                 of table in the column c, for every
//                 0 <= c <= table.numcols() - 1

{
    int r, c;
    int nRows = table.numrows();
    int nCols = table.numcols();

    total.resize(nCols);

    for (c = 0; c < nCols; c++)
    {
        total[c] = 0.;
        for (r = 0; r < nRows; r++)
            total[c] += table[r][c];
    }
}
```

The above function shows how the `numrows()` and `numcols()` functions can be used to obtain the dimensions of a matrix and how subscripts are used to access matrix elements.

As with the `apvector` class, the `apmatrix` class makes run-time checks that subscript values fall within the valid range and terminates with an error message if a subscript is out of bounds.

To summarize:

- `apmatrix` arguments should always be passed to functions by reference, or by constant reference if that argument is not changed in the function.
- The `numrows()` and `numcols()` member functions return the number of rows and columns in the matrix, respectively.
- The `resize(int newRows, int newCols)` member function sets the dimensions of the matrix to given non-negative numbers. It is important to make sure that the dimensions are set before you use the matrix.
- You can access individual elements of a matrix using two subscripts, in the same way as for standard two-dimensional arrays: `m[r][c]`. Both subscripts start from 0. An element with a subscript may be an *rvalue* or an *lvalue*, that is, it may appear either on the right- or left-hand side of the assignment operator.
- The assignment operator for matrices appropriately resizes the destination matrix and copies the right-hand-side operand into it.

15

Consider the following code segment:

```
apmatrix<char> m;
int k;

for (k = 0; k < m.numrows(); k++)
{
    m[k][m.numcols()-1] = '*';
}
```

Which of the following best describes the result when this code segment is executed?

(A)   All elements in the first row are set to `'*'`.
(B)   All elements in the last row are set to `'*'`.
(C)   All elements in the last column are set to `'*'`.
(D)   The code has no effect.
(E)   Subscript-out-of-bounds error is reported.

Cheap trick! `m` is declared as an empty matrix with dimensions 0, 0. The `for` loop is never entered because `m.numcols()` returns 0. The answer is D.

apvector and apmatrix: reading from files

There are no special functions for reading a whole vector or a whole matrix from `cin` or from a file. You have to read each element separately. For example:

```
for (k = 0; k < v.length(); k++)
{
    cin >> v[k];
}
```
Or:
```
for (r = 0; k < m.numrows(); r++)
{
    for (c = 0; c < m.numcols(); c++)
    {
        inFile >> m[r][c];
    }
}
```

The `>>` operator automatically skips all white space: spaces, tabs, and line breaks.

There are many more examples of code using the `apvector` and `apmatrix` classes in the practice free-response questions (Chapter 5).

2.5. Strings, the `apstring` Class

> **In all AP materials, character strings are represented either by literal strings in double quotes or by `apstring` variables.**

The following are examples of valid string declarations:

```
apstring name;                  // Declares an empty string
apstring city = "San Diego";    // Declares a string equal to "San Diego"
apstring city1("San Diego");    // Same thing
apstring city2 = city;          // Declares a string and initializes it
                                //    to a copy of a previously defined string
apstring city3(city2);          // The same as: apstring city3 = city2;
```

Note that there is no way to declare a string of a given length, other than initializing it to a literal string of that length. Nor there is a way to explicitly resize a string.

> **The apstring class does not have the `resize` function. Strings are resized automatically when they are copied, concatenated, or read from `cin` or from files.**

> **Strings should be passed to functions by reference or by constant reference.**

You can access the individual characters in a string using subscripts, which are checked for valid range. In addition, the `apstring` class supports the following operators and member functions:

`=`	Copies one string into another.
`+`	Concatenates two strings or a string and a `char`.
`+=`	Appends a string or a `char` to the left-hand-side string.
`==, !=, <, >, <=, >=`	Compares strings alphabetically (case sensitive).
`int length()`	Returns the length of the string.
`int find(ch)` `int find(str)`	Return the position of the first occurrence of the given character or the given substring. Return a constant `npos`, (no position) if not found.
`apstring` `substr(pos, len);`	Builds and returns a substring of length `len` starting at `pos`.
`istream &` `getline(is, str)`	Reads one line from an input stream `is` (`cin` or a file) into `str`.

Let's try to cram it all together into one example. The following function checks if the next line in a file has the form `#include <...>` and, if so, prints the name inside the angular brackets:

```
void PrintIncludes (istream & inFile)
{
    apstring line;
    int pos1, pos2, len;

    getline(inFile, line);
    if (line.length() >= 8 && line.substr(0, 8) == "#include")
    {
        pos1 = line.find('<');
        pos2 = line.find('>');
        if (pos1 != npos && pos2 != npos)
        {
            len = pos2 - pos1 - 1;    // Number of chars inside <...>
            if (len > 0)
                cout << line.substr(pos1 + 1, len) << endl;

        // Or, instead of the above three lines:
        // int k;
        // for (k = pos1 + 1; k < pos2; k++) cout << line[k];
        // cout << endl;
        }
    }
}
```

16

Consider the following function:

```
int MysteryCount(const apstring & str)
{
    int count = 0;
    int k;

    for (k = 0; k < str.length(); k++)
    {
        if (str[k] == 'x')
        {
            count++;
        }
        else if (str[k] == 'o')
        {
            count--;
        }
        else
        {
            count = 0;
        }
    }
    return count;
}
```

What is the return value when `MysteryCount("oooxx-xxooo")` is called?

(A)   -2
(B)   -1
(C)   0
(D)   1
(E)   2

☞ This function pretends that it calculates the difference between the number of *x*'s and the number of *o*'s in the string, but count is reset back to 0 after each character that is not an *x* or an *o*. So the real counting starts at the last run of *x*'s / *o*'s. This has two *x*'s and three *o*'s; the count is -1. The answer is B. ☚

2.6. Structures and Classes

Classes and structures combine data members with member functions.

You should know the following concepts and terms: *private* and *public* members, *constructor* and *destructor*, *default constructor*, *initializer list*.

Class or structure members, both data and functions, may be *public* or *private*.

Public members are accessible anywhere in the code; private members are accessible only within the `class` member functions.

The only difference between `struct` and `class` is that in a class the first group of members is by default <u>private</u>, unless specifically marked `public`. In AP materials, the public members of a class are usually listed first. In a `struct`, the first group of members is by default <u>public</u>. Usually <u>all</u> members of a structure are public.

A class or a structure introduces a user-defined data type into the program. Each class or `struct` may have one or several *constructors* and one *destructor*. The constructors determine all the valid forms of declarations of constants and variables for the data type associated with the class or structure.

The appropriate constructor is called automatically when a variable is declared or allocated. The destructor is called automatically when the variable goes out of scope or is deallocated.

Normally, we want to be able to declare a variable without any initialization. For that we need a constructor that doesn't take any arguments.

A constructor that does not take any arguments is called the *default constructor*.

Constructors and destructors are always public member functions. The name of all constructors is the same as the name of the class or structure and the same as the name of the data type that it defines. The name of the destructor is the same, preceded by ~.

Constructors and destructors do not have any return data type, not even `void`.

If no constructors are specified, the compiler supplies the "automatic" version. The automatic constructor just reserves memory for the class or `struct` variable. The automatic destructor releases that memory.

Consider the following structure:

```
struct Fraction
{
    int numerator;
    int denominator;

    Fraction();              // Default constructor (no arguments)
    Fraction(int a, int b);  // Constructor with two arguments
                             // No destructor -- "automatic" version is used
};
```

The above structure has two constructors that correspond to the following two ways of declaring a `Fraction` variable:

```
Fraction f1;        // Uses the default constructor (with no arguments)
Fraction f2(2,3);   // Uses the second constructor, which takes two arguments
```

The code for these two constructors may be as follows:

```
Fraction::Fraction()
{
    numerator = 1;
    denominator = 1;
}

Fraction::Fraction(int a, int b)
{
    numerator = a;
    denominator = b;
}
```

The same constructors may be coded using an *initializer list*:

```
Fraction::Fraction()
  : numerator(1), denominator(1)
{} // Empty body: all the work is done by the initializer list

Fraction::Fraction(int a, int b)
  : numerator(a), denominator(b)
{}
```

Initializer lists are indispensable when a class or a struct has apvector, apmatrix, or apstring members that need to be initialized. For example:

```
struct Club
{
    apstring clubName;
    int numMembers;
    apvector<apstring> clubMembers;

    Club(const apstring & name, int num);
    // Constructor, builds a Club with a given name
    //    and a capacity to hold a given number of club members
};

// Implementation:

Club::Club(const apstring & name, int num)
  : clubName(name), numMembers(0), clubMembers(num)
{}
```

In the above initializer list, clubMembers(num) sets the size of the vector; this is the preferred way of doing so, as opposed to placing a call to clubMembers.resize(num) inside the constructor's body.

Traditionally, all the members of a structure are public and a structure usually does not include member functions, with the exception, perhaps, of one or two constructors. A class may be more involved.

In addition to constructors, you need to know the following concepts and terms related to classes: *encapsulation, accessor, modifier, const member function, overloaded member functions, client.*

Consider the Club example rewritten as a class:

```
class Club
{
  public:

    Club(const apstring & name, int num);      // Constructor
    int GetNumberOfMembers() const;            // Accessor
    void SetClubName(const apstring & name);   // Modifier
    void Remove(const apstring & memberName);
    void Remove(int k);

  private:

    apstring myClubName;
    int myNumMembers;
    apvector<apstring> myClubMembers;
};
```

The above is called the *class definition*. The actual code for member functions is called the *class implementation*. Here is an example of the code for the three functions:

```
// Implementation:

Club::Club(const apstring & name, int num)              // Constructor
   : myClubName(name), myNumMembers(0), myClubMembers(num)
{}

int Club::GetNumberOfMembers() const                    // Accessor
{
    return myNumMembers;
}

void Club::SetClubName(const apstring & name)           // Modifier
{
    myClubName = name;
}
```

Note the following features in this example:

1. All data members of the class are made private. This limits access to class's data members outside the class forcing programmers to use provided member functions for interfacing the class — a technique known as *encapsulation*.

2. All data members have names that start with the prefix "my." This is the style in all AP materials; it makes a class's data members easily identifiable and their names different from the names of local variables and function arguments.

3. One of the public member functions, GetNumberOfMembers(...), returns myNumMembers. Such a function may be needed because myNumMembers is a private member and functions outside the class (which are not this class's members) do not have direct access to it. Member functions of this type are called *accessors*. Accessors do not change data members of the class; this fact is documented and enforced by adding the keyword const in the function's declaration after its list of arguments.

4. The other public member function, SetClubName(...), is provided so that we can change the myClubName member. Functions that change one or several members of a class are called *modifiers*. Naturally, modifiers cannot be const.

5. The class has two versions of the Remove member function: one takes an apstring (presumably a club member's name) as an argument, the other takes an integer (presumably a position in the club member list) as an argument. Member functions that have the same name but take different numbers or types of arguments are called *overloaded* functions.

The "accessor" and "modifier" designations are somewhat informal — a class may have a member function that sets some data members to new values and at the same time returns, say, their old values or the values of other members. A class may have a `const` member function that doesn't change the data members, but it may build and return something too complicated to be properly called an accessor.

The compiler treats overloaded functions as different functions; the compiler figures out which one to call based on the number and types of the arguments in the call.

In an encapsulated class all data members are private and some member functions may be private — they are used only by other member functions. Public member functions may be called anywhere.

Functions and modules that call public member functions of a class are called *clients* of the class.

Dot notation for accessing members

Public members of a class or a structure, both data members and member functions, are accessed in client programs using "dot" notation.

For example:

```
Club computer("Computer", 35);
...
int num = computer.GetNumberOfMembers();
```

⌈ In the AB exam, structures that represent nodes of a linked list or a tree are addressed through pointers and their members are accessed using the "arrow" notation. For example:

```
TreeNode * root;   // A pointer to the root node
...
apstring data  = root->info;
```

17

Consider the following class declaration:

```
class Date
{
  public:
    Date();
    Date(const apstring & monthName, int day, int year);
    void SetDate(int month, int day, int year);
    < other public member functions not shown >

  private:
    < private members not shown >
};
```

Consider modifying the Date class so that it is possible to initialize variables of the type Date with month, day, year information when they are declared, as well as to set their values later using the member function SetDate(...). For example, the following code should define and initialize three Date type variables.

```
Date d1;
d1.SetDate("January", 1, 2000);
Date d2("December", 31, 1999);
Date d3(12, 31, 1999);
```

Which of the following best describes the additional member functions that should be provided?

(A)   An overloaded version of SetDate with three int arguments
(B)   An overloaded version of SetDate with one apstring and two int arguments
(C)   A constructor with three int arguments
(D)   Both an overloaded version of SetDate with three int arguments and a constructor with three int arguments
(E)   Both an overloaded version of SetDate with one apstring and two int arguments and a constructor with three int arguments

☞ This is a verbose but simple question. Just match the declarations against the provided class features:

```
Date d1; ──────────────────── Date();
d1.SetDate("January", 1, 2000);─┐ ┌─Date(apstring, int, int);
 Date d2("December", 31, 1999); ─┤ X  void SetDate(int, int, int);
 Date d3(12, 31, 1999); ──────── ┘ └ Missing Date(int, int, int);
                                     └ Missing SetDate(apstring, int, int);
```

As we can see, a version of SetDate with apstring and two int arguments and a constructor with three int arguments are missing. The answer is E. ☜

Questions 18-21 refer to the following class declaration:

```
class TicketSales
{
  public:

    TicketSales(const apstring & movieName);

    void SetWeekSales(int week, double dollars);
    // Sets box office receipts for a given week

    void PrintBestWeek() const;
    // Finds and returns the week with best sales
    < Other public members not shown >

  private:

    apstring myName;
    apvector<double> mySales;
              // mySales[0], ..., mySales[51] hold sales
              //    totals for 52 weeks
    int FindBestWeek() const;
};
```

18

The function `FindBestWeek` is NOT a public member function because

(A)   `FindBestWeek` is not intended to be used by clients of the class
(B)   `FindBestWeek` is intended to be used only by clients of the class
(C)   Functions that work with private data members of the `apvector` type cannot be public
(D)   Functions that have a loop in their code cannot be public
(E)   Functions that return a value cannot be public

☞ In this question only the first two choices deserve any consideration — the other three are fillers. You might get confused for a moment about what a "client" means, but common sense helps: a client is anyone who is not yourself, so if a client needs to use something of yours, you have to make it public. Private things are for yourself, not for clients. The answer is A. ☜

19

The constructor for the `TicketSales` class uses an initializer list to set the name of a movie to a given string and the size of the `apvector mySales` to 52:

```
TicketSales::TicketSales(const apstring & movieName)
: < initializer list >
{}
```

Which of the following is the appropriate choice for the < *initializer list* >?

(A)   `movieName, mySales[52]`
(B)   `myName(movieName), mySales(52)`
(C)   `myName(movieName), mySales.resize(52)`
(D)   `(movieName, 52)`
(E)   `movieName, mySales.length() = 52`

☞ An initializer list associates some (not necessarily all) class data members with given values. It has to tell explicitly which member gets which value, and the correct syntax for it appears in B. An initializer list can call functions, but it is unlikely that in AP questions an initializer list will include any function calls. The answer is B. ☜

20

The member function `PrintBestWeek` in the `TicketSales` class is designated `const` because

(A)   It has output operators in it
(B)   It does not change the size of the apvector `mySales`
(C)   It does not change any private members of the class
(D)   It does not change any data members of the class
(E)   It calls a `const` function, `FindBestWeek`

☞ A member function should be designated `const` if it does not change any data members of the class (i.e., D). But this may be a tricky question because other answers, except B, may sound plausible, too. Take A for example: a function that displays a class object most likely doesn't change it, so it's likely to be designated `const`. But there is no such law that a function cannot change the object just because it has a couple of output operators in it. In an encapsulated class all data members are private, so C sounds reasonable. But the question does not stipulate that the `TicketSales` class is encapsulated; what if it has a public data member? Consider E: it is true that if a `const` function calls another member function, the called function must be `const`, too. But the converse is not true: `PrintBestWeek` doesn't have to be `const` just because it calls `FindBestweek`, which is designated `const`. Always choose the most general correct hypothesis. The answer is D. ☜

21

Given the definition

```
TicketSales movie("Titanic");
```

which of the following statements sets the third week sales for that movie to 245,000?

(A)   `movie = TicketSales(3, 245000.00);`
(B)   `SetWeekSales(movie, 3, 245000.00);`
(C)   `movie.SetWeekSales(3, 245000.00);`
(D)   `movie(SetWeekSales, 3, 245000.00);`
(E)   `SetWeekSales(3, 245000.00);`

☞ The variable `movie` of the type `TicketSales` is defined outside the class, in a client of the class. The key word in this question is "sets." It indicates that a member function, a modifier, is called, and the way to call a member function from a client is with dot notation. (Besides, A assumes that there is a constructor with two arguments; B and D look like calls to non-existing functions; E forgets to mention `movie` altogether.) The answer is C. ↵

2.7. Templated Functions and Classes and Overloaded Functions

Functions with the same name but different numbers or types of arguments are called *overloaded* functions. Overloaded functions are either all members of the same class or are all free-standing functions (i.e., not members of any class).

The compiler treats overloaded functions as different functions. It figures out which one to call depending on the form of the call.

The `apstring` class, for example, has two forms of the `find` member function:

```
int find(const apstring & str);   // e.g. msg.find("hello") or msg.find(word);
int find(char ch);                // e.g. msg.find('!') or msg.find(letter);
```

These are overloaded member functions.

Now consider two forms of a Swap function — one swaps ints, the other apstrings:

```
void Swap(int & a, int & b)                 // Swap two integers
{
    int temp = a; a = b; b = temp;
}

void Swap(apstring & s1, apstring & s2)    // Swap two strings
{
    apstring temp = s1; s1 = s2; s2 = temp;
}
```

These are overloaded free-standing functions.

Overloaded functions shouldn't be confused with *templated* functions that work with multiple data types. For example, the above Swap function can be written as a template that works with any reasonable data type:

```
template <class anyType>
void Swap(anyType & a, anyType & b)
{
    anyType temp = a; a = b; b = temp;
}
```

In the above code, anyType is a parameter that can become int, double, apstring, and so on, depending on how the function is used.

A whole class may be written as a template. The apvector class, for example, is a templated class that supports arrays with elements of any data type.

22

Which of the following best describes the reasons for using a set of overloaded functions that work with several data types as opposed to implementing one templated function that works with these data types?

    I.   Easier to maintain the program
    II.   Better run-time performance
    III.   Different algorithms are required for different data types

(A)   I only
(B)   II only
(C)   III only
(D)   I and II
(E)   II and III

☞ It is usually easier to maintain a program with one function rather than many, so Reason I is false. Reason II is irrelevant: the performance is the same. But Reason III is true: if different data types require different algorithms, how can you put all of them into one templated function? You need to overload. The answer is C. ↵

2.8. Overloaded Operators

C++ allows you to change or define new meanings of standard operators (=, <, +, <<, !, etc.) for user-defined data types. This is called *operator overloading*. An operator is overloaded by defining a new function operator*X*, where *X* is one of the C++ operator symbols.

Coding overloaded operators is not required for the A exam.

An operator can be overloaded as a member of a class or as a free-standing operator.

When a binary operator is overloaded as a free-standing operator, its two arguments serve as the operands. In this case,

```
z = x + y;
```

is basically the same as

```
z = operator+ (x, y);
```

When a binary operator is overloaded as a class member, the object itself serves as the first operand and its one argument as the second operand. In this case,

```
z = x + y;
```

is the same as

```
z = x.operator+ (y);
```

The advantage of overloading as a member is that the operator has ready access to the private members of the class. The limitation is that the first (left-hand-side) operand must be always of the type of that class.

Member vs. free-standing operator overloading often depends on the operator type. This is discussed below for common operators.

_____ Overloading operators = and += _____

An overloaded assignment operator may be needed for your structure or class when the default member-by-member assignment does not do the job. This may happen, for example, when your structure or class has a pointer to a dynamically allocated array, as in apstring or apvector classes.

Assignment and compound assignment operators are usually implemented as members.

For example:

```
class Fraction
{
  public:
    Fraction(int a, int b);              // Constructor

    const Fraction & operator+= (int x);   // Overloaded +=
    ...

  private:
    int myNumer;
    int myDenom;

    void Reduce();
    ...
};
```

In the Fraction class above, overloaded = operator is not needed as standard, member-by-member assignment does the job. The += operator adds an integer to a fraction. It can be used as follows:

```
Fraction ratio;
int x;
...
ratio += x;
```

By convention, the return type of assignment and compound assignment operators is a constant reference to the same class, const SomeClass &, and they return a reference to the same object, which is represented by *this. this is a C++ reserved word. For example:

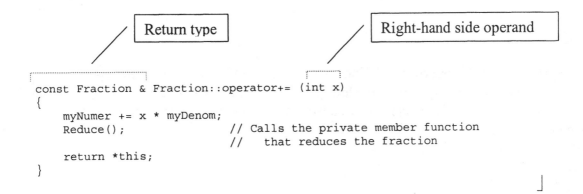

```
const Fraction & Fraction::operator+= (int x)
{
    myNumer += x * myDenom;
    Reduce();                  // Calls the private member function
                               //    that reduces the fraction
    return *this;
}
```

A class may have several forms of overloaded operators. For example:

```
const Fraction & operator+= (int x);
const Fraction & operator+= (const Fraction & f);
```

Overloading >> and <<

The input and output operators, >> and <<, are always overloaded as free-standing operators because their left-hand-side operand is `istream` or `ostream` respectively, not the given class type.

This creates a problem with access to private members which in the AP materials is resolved by adding, when necessary, a public helper member function that does the work. The >> and << operators by convention return a reference to the same stream. For example:

```
ostream & operator<< (ostream & os, const Date & date)
{
    date.Print(os);   // Calls a public member function
                      //    that outputs date to os
    return os;
}
```

Overloading +, etc.

Other binary operators may be implemented as members or non-members depending on their use. For example, the overloaded + operator for the `apstring` class is overloaded as a non-member because we want to be able to use a `char` as the first argument, which is not the class type.

```
apstring msg, starMsg;
...
starMsg = '*' + msg;     // '*' is not apstring type (it's the char type)
```

23

Suppose a class `Fraction` has defined overloaded = and += member operators. The +=
operator adds a given fraction to the left-hand side. Which one of the following segments
of code correctly implements an overloaded + operator that adds two fractions and
returns the resulting fraction?

(A)

```
const & Fraction operator+ (const Fraction & f1, const Fraction & f2)
{
    Fraction sum = f1;
    sum += f2;
    return sum;
}
```

(B)

```
Fraction operator+ (const Fraction & f1, const Fraction & f2)
{
    Fraction sum = f1;
    sum += f2;
    return sum;
}
```

(C)

```
const Fraction & operator+ (const Fraction & f1, const Fraction & f2)
{
    Fraction sum = f1;
    sum += f2;
    return *this;
}
```

(D)

```
const Fraction & operator+ (const Fraction & f1, const Fraction & f2)
{
    return f1 += f2;
}
```

(E)

```
Fraction Fraction::operator+ (const Fraction & f2)
{
    *this += f2;
    return *this;
}
```

☞ This is the kind of question you might be tempted to skip! In fact, it's not so difficult.
First, note that the operator has to build and return a new fraction, not a reference to some
existing fraction. This eliminates A, C, and D, which all have an & in the return type.
The A solution is the most harmful — it returns a reference to a local variable, always a
bad idea. C has a syntax error, because this version overloads + as a non-member, so
`this` is undefined. D has two problems: it changes `f1`, which is designated `const`, and
it returns a reference to `f1` instead of creating a new object. E seems plausible, but it has
what is called a *side effect*: in addition to returning the sum it adds `f2` to the first operand.
The correct method is B: it defines a new fraction, `sum`, sets it to `f1 + f2` using the
provided member operators = and +=, and returns its <u>value</u> (not a reference). The answer
is B. ☜

2.9. Input and Output

In the AP subset, input is limited to reading from `cin` or from a text file using the `>>` operator or the `getline` function for `apstrings`. Output is limited to using the `<<` operator. You may need `endl`, but no other formatting. Functions that open files or check the status of the input or output streams won't be tested. It is always assumed that the input or the file has valid information, so no additional data validation is required unless specifically requested in the question.

The `>>` operator can read one item from `cin` or from a file: a number, a character, a word. It skips all the "white space" (spaces, tabs, newline characters, etc.) before the item and stops reading when it gets the requested information (e.g., a number, one non-space character, or one word). For example, the file may have the following text:

```
Mary C. Fields
15
```

You can read this information as follows:

```
apstring firstName, lastName;
char middleInitial, dot;
int age;

inFile >> firstName >> middleInitial >> dot >> lastName >> age;
```

You can also read the whole line into an `apstring`, white space and all:

```
apstring name;

getline(inFile, name);  // Now the apstring name contains Mary C. Fields
```

In the following example, data for a picture is stored in a text file with the first line holding the dimensions of the picture (the number of rows and columns) and subsequent lines holding the picture itself. This is similar to the 1999 "Quilt" question from the free-response section of the exam. The file may look like this:

```
3 5
x...x
xxxxx
....x
```

Suppose you have a class `Picture` defined with a constructor that initializes the picture by reading its dimensions and the picture elements from a given file. You have to supply the code for this constructor. The precondition is that the file is open for reading — a typical situation since the AP questions do not deal with opening files.

```
class Picture
{
  public:

    Picture(istream & inFile);
    ...

  private:

    int myNumRows;
    int myNumCols;
    apmatrix<char> myPixels;
};
```

There are two ways to implement this constructor, an easy way and a hard way. The easy way is just to read all the information using the >> operator:

```
Picture::Picture(istream & inFile)
// precondition:  inFile is a text file open for reading.
// postcondition: myNumRows and myNumCols are initialized to the values
//                read from the file.  apmatrix myPixels is resized and
//                initialized to the picture elements read from the file.
//                inFile is left open after reading the picture information.
{
    int r, c;

    inFile >> myNumRows >> myNumCols;
    myPixels.resize(myNumRows, myNumCols);

    for (r = 0; r < myNumRows; r++)
        for (c = 0; c < myNumCols; c++)
            inFile >> myPixels[r][c];
}
```

It is important to resize the myPixels matrix before reading into it. It is also important to read from the given file, not from cin.

The hard way is to read the picture data line by line:

```
Picture::Picture(istream & inFile)
{
    int r, c;
    apstring rowData;

    inFile >> myNumRows >> myNumCols;
    inFile.ignore(100, '\n');            // Skip the rest of the line
                                         //   (not part of the AP subset)
    myPixels.resize(myNumRows, myNumCols);

    for (r = 0; r < myNumRows; r++)
    {
        getline(inFile, rowData);
        for (c = 0; c < myNumCols; c++)
            myPixels[r][c] = rowData[c];
    }
}
```

The >> operator reads data elements from the input stream, but it leaves the *newline* character in the stream. In the first solution, the subsequent calls to >> skip the newline characters as well as all other white space characters. This solution works only because the picture data do not include spaces. The second solution is more general, but you have to be more careful: it is important to consume the newline character after reading myNumRows and myNumCols. This is accomplished here by calling the ignore function, which, strictly speaking, is not in the AP subset. Alternatively, you can use one dummy call to getline. If you forget to call ignore or to get rid of the newline character in some other way and try to read a data line, the first call to getline will give you an empty string instead.

Output

Output may use only the << operator and the endl manipulator. For example, a member function Print can be added to the Picture class to write the picture data into a file, in the same format as the original input data file:

```
void Picture::Print(ostream & outFile) const
// precondition:  outFile is open for writing.
// postcondition: Picture data are written to the file.
{
    int r, c;

    outFile << myNumRows << ' ' << myNumCols << endl;
    for (r = 0; r < myNumRows; r++)
    {
        for (c = 0; c < myNumCols; c++)
            outFile << myPixels[r][c];
        outFile << endl;
    }
}
```

Note that the << operator does not automatically separate the output elements — you need to insert spaces or endl yourself.

We could use the Print function to overload the << operator for the Picture class:

```
ostream & operator<< (ostream & outFile, const Picture & pic)
{
    pic.Print(outFile);
    return outFile;
}
```

The Print member function is needed here because, as explained in Section 2.8, the << operator is always overloaded as a free-standing operator with no access to the private members of the class.

Chapter 3. Exam Topics: Program Design, Data Structures, and Algorithms

3.1. Computer Systems

You are probably aware by now that a typical computer system's <u>hardware</u> has at least one *processor*, (a.k.a. CPU), *RAM* (*random-access memory*), secondary storage devices (such as magnetic disks, CD-ROM drives, floppy disk drives, etc.) and *peripherals* (modems, printers, sound cards and speakers, mice or other pointing devices, etc.).

Chances are you also have worked with an *operating system*, a piece of <u>software</u> that controls the computer system and interacts with a user. MS DOS, Windows 98, and Linux are examples of operating systems. A *compiler* is also a piece of software. It checks syntax in programs written in a high-level programming language and translates them into machine code. In a modular language, like C++, you can compile individual modules separately, creating *object* modules. A *linker*, another program, combines several object modules and builds an executable program. A *debugger* is a program that helps you run and test your program in a controlled way and find errors ("bugs") in it. The editor, compiler, linker, debugger, and other *software development tools* may be combined in one package called *IDE* (Integrated Development Environment) with a *GUI* (graphical user interface).

The issues of system reliability and security and legal and ethical issues related to computer use are not precisely defined in the AP exam guidelines. Questions about these things would have to be rather general.

3.2. Program Design and Development Methodology

Computer science courses try to emphasize *problem solving*, as opposed to just programming in a particular language or using specific hardware platforms. The exam topics related to general software design and development methodology emphasize *procedural abstraction*, *data abstraction*, and *reusability* of code. Here is a very brief glossary of the relevant terms:

Specifications — a detailed description of what a piece of software should accomplish and how it should behave and interact with the user. Specifications may be given for a whole system, one module, even one function or class.

Top-down design — the design methodology where you first define the general structure of the program, high-level tasks or modules and their interaction. Then you refine the design of each task, identify subtasks and smaller modules, classes or functions. Then you refine the design of subtasks, individual functions and so on.

Top-down development — similar to top-down design: you first lay out your code at a high level, defining general functions and classes. These functions may call lower-level functions, which are not yet implemented. You can compile and sometimes even test high-level pieces of your code by substituting "stubs" — empty or greatly simplified versions — for still uncoded low-level functions.

Bottom-up development — in this method you start development with low-level structures and functions that are needed for your project (and hopefully will be *reusable* in other projects). You then implement higher-level structures and functions that rely on already implemented lower-level modules, and so on, building a system of hierarchically organized modules starting from its foundation.

Data structure — combines a method for data organization with methods of accessing and manipulating the data. For example, a two-dimensional array with functions or operators for retrieving and changing the values of its elements is a data structure that may be useful for representing tables.

Abstract data type (ADT) — an abstract description of a data structure that emphasizes its properties and functionality as opposed to specific implementation. For example, the *Queue* ADT may be described as a structure for storing a list of data elements with functions for inserting and removing an element in such a way that a new element is always inserted at the end of the list and an element is always retrieved and removed from the beginning of the list.

Procedural abstraction — a description of a procedure that is not tied to a specific hardware platform, data types, and other details. A high-level programming language, such as C++, already assures a degree of procedural abstraction by isolating a programmer from a particular hardware platform. Templated functions and classes in C++ allow a programmer to implement algorithms and functions that will work for different data types — another level of abstraction. An algorithm may be described using pseudocode, flowcharts, and other tools that make the description even more abstract, independent of any particular programming language.

Reusable code — debugged and tested fragments of code or software modules (e.g., sets of functions, classes) that are somewhat general in nature and can be reused in other projects.

Modular development and testing — modern programming languages, such as C++, allow you to split functions and classes between different modules. A module can be compiled and tested separately before it is integrated into the whole system.

User interface — the behavior of a program as it interacts with users: screens, menus, commands, messages, graphics, sounds, and so on.

These are very general concepts and it is not easy to come up with multiple-choice or free-response questions that test in-depth understanding of these concepts. In past exams, design and implementation questions were limited to specific data structures and algorithms. These are reviewed in Section 3.8.

3.3. Iterations

Most programming languages provide iteration control structures, such as the `while`, `for`, and `do-while` loops in C++. Simple loops are good for iterating (repeating the same operation) over a range of numbers or over the elements of a one-dimensional array ⌈ or a linked list ⌋.

A `for` loop is a convenient and idiomatic way to *traverse* a one-dimensional array:

```
int k, len = A.length();

for (k = 0; k < len; k++)
{
    cout << A[k] << endl;      // ... or do whatever you need to do
                               //     with each element
}
```

For working with two-dimensional arrays you usually need *nested* loops. The following code, for example, traverses a two-dimensional array represented by an `apmatrix M`:

```
int r, c;

for (r = 0; r < M.numrows(); r++)
{
    for (c = 0; c < M.numcols(); c++)
    {
        cout << M[r][c] << ' ';   // ... or do whatever...
    }
    cout << endl;
}
```

Note that braces are optional if the body of the loop has only one statement:

```
for (r = 0; r < M.numrows(); r++)
    for (c = 0; c < M.numcols(); c++)
        if (M[r][c] <= 0)
            return true;
```

In a "triangular" nested loop the outer loop may run, say, for *i* from 1 to *n* and the inner loop may run for *j* from 0 to *i*-1. The following nested loops, for example, transpose a square matrix (i.e., flip it symmetrically over its main diagonal):

```
int n = M.numrows();

for (i = 1; i < n; i++)
    for (j = 0; j < i; j++)
        Swap(M[i][j], M[j][i]);
```

Here the inner loop runs *i* times for *i* = 1, ..., *n*-1, so the total number of swaps is

$$1 + 2 + ... + (n-1) = \frac{n(n-1)}{2}$$

The AB exam material includes linked list traversals. A `for` loop can be used for that, too:

```
Node * p;
for (p = head; p != NULL; p = p->next)
{
    cout << p->info << endl;
}
```

Max and Min

A common example of using loops is finding a maximum or a minimum value (or its position) in an array:

```
double Max(const apvector<double> & A, int n)
// precondition:  Array A holds values A[0], ..., A[n-1]; n >= 1
// postcondition: Returns maxValue such that maxValue >= A[k]
//                for any 0 <= k <= n-1 and maxValue = A[k] for some k.
{
    double maxValue = A[0];
    int k;

    for (k = 1; k < n; k++)
    {
        if (A[k] > maxValue)
            maxValue = A[k];
    }
    return maxValue;
}
```

24

What does the following function do?

```
double MinOrMax(const apmatrix<double> & M)
{
    double x = 0., y;
    int r, c;

    for (c = 0; c < M.numcols(); c++)
    {
        y = M[0][c];
        for (r = 1; r < M.numrows(); r++)
            if (M[r][c] > y)
                y = M[r][c];
        if (c == 0 || y < x)
            x = y;
    }
    return x;
}
```

(A)   Returns the smallest value in M
(B)   Returns the largest value in M
(C)   Finds the maximum value in each column in M and returns the smallest of them
(D)   Finds the minimum value in each column in M and returns the largest of them
(E)   Finds the maximum value in the first column in M and the minimum value in all other columns and returns the smallest of the two

☞ A and B must be wrong: too much is going on. The inner loop clearly finds the maximum value in column c and places it in y. The outer loop sets x for the first column and updates it, if necessary, to find the minimum. The answer is C. ☟

25

Consider the following function:

```
double MaxSum(const apvector<double> & A, int n)
// precondition:  n >= 2.  A[0] ... A[n-1] are filled with values.
// postcondition: Returns the largest sum of any two different elements.
{
    < code >
}
```

Which of the following code segments can replace < *code* > so that the function works as specified?

I.
```
double max = A[0] + A[1];
int i, j;

for (i = 1; i < n; i++)
    for (j = 0; j < i; j++)
        if (A[i] + A[j] > max)
            max = A[i] + A[j];
return max;
```

II.
```
double max1 = A[0], max2 = A[0];
int i;

for (i = 1; i < n; i++)
    if (A[i] > max1)
        max1 = A[i];

for (i = 1; i < n; i++)
    if (A[i] != max1 && A[i] > max2)
        max2 = A[i];

return max1 + max2;
```

III.
```
double max1 = A[0], max2 = A[1];
int i;

if (A[1] > A[0])
{
    max1 = A[1];
    max2 = A[0];
}

for (i = 2; i < n; i++)
{
    if (A[i] > max1)
    {
        max2 = max1;
        max1 = A[i];
    }
    else if (A[i] > max2)
        max2 = A[i];
}

return max1 + max2;
```

(A)   I only
(B)   II only
(C)   I and II
(D)   I and III
(E)   I, II, and III

This is a lot of code for one question, unless you know exactly what's going on. Segment I is inefficient but most straightforward: using triangular nested loops we generate sums for all the different pairs of elements and choose the largest of them. Segment II is based on a different idea: to find the largest value, then the second largest value in two separate traversals of the array. But it has two problems. First, if the largest value happens to be A[0], the second `for` loop will never update max2. Second, it will fail if the largest value appears in the array more than once. The postcondition states that the function is looking for the largest sum of two different elements, not two different values. This approach could work, though, with a couple of minor fixes:

```
int iMax1 = 0, iMax2 = 0;
int i;

for (i = 1; i < n; i++)
    if (A[i] > A[iMax1])
        iMax1 = i;

if (iMax1 == 0)
    iMax2 = 1;

for (i = 1; i < n; i++)
    if (i != iMax1 && A[i] > A[iMax2])
        iMax2 = i;

return A[iMax1] + A[iMax2];
```

In Segment III we find both the largest and the second largest elements in one sweep. Note how the largest element becomes second largest when we find one with a greater value. It works fine. The answer is D.

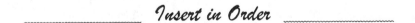

Insert in Order

Many applications, including Insertion Sort, require you to insert an element into a sorted array while preserving the order:

```
void InsertInOrder(apvector<int> & A, int n, int newValue)
// precondition:  A[0] <= A[1] <= ... <= A[n-1].  n < A.length()
// postcondition: Elements A[k], ..., A[n-1] are shifted
//                appropriately into A[k+1], ..., A[n] and
//                newValue is inserted into A[k] so that the ascending order
//                is preserved.
{
    int k;

    // Shift elements to the right by one until you find the
    //      place to insert:

    for (k = n; k > 0; k--)      // Start at the end
    {
        if (A[k-1] <= newValue)
            break;
        else
            A[k] = A[k-1];       // Shift by one towards the end of the array
    }
    A[k] = newValue;
}
```

In the above code we shift the elements in the array to the right by one to create a vacant slot and then insert the new value into the created vacancy. Note that the shifting has to proceed from the end, so that each shifted element is placed into a vacant slot and does not overwrite any data before it is used (see Figure 3-1). Don't forget to resize the apvector first if all of its elements are used:

```
void InsertInOrder(apvector<int> & A, int newValue)
{
    int n = A.length();
    int k;

    A.resize(n+1);

    // Shift elements ...
    for (k = n; k > 0; k--)
        ...
}
```

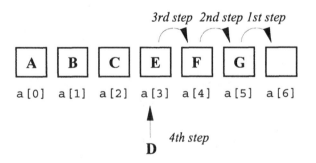

Figure 3-1. Inserting a new value in the middle of an array

26

Consider an array A that contains n integer elements sorted in ascending order
(n < A.length()). Which of the following code segments correctly inserts newValue
into A, so that the ascending order is preserved?

I.
```
int k;
for (k = n; k > 0; k--)
{
    if (A[k-1] <= newValue)
    {
        A[k] = newValue;
        break;
    }
    else
        A[k] = A[k-1];
}
```

II.
```
int k = n;
while (k > 0 && A[k-1] > newValue)
{
    A[k] = A[k-1];
    k--;
}
A[k] = newValue;
```

III.
```
int j, k;
for (k = 0; k < n; k++)
{
    if (A[k] >= newValue)
        break;
}
for (j = n-1; j >= k; j--)
{
    A[j+1] = A[j];
}
A[k] = newValue;
```

(A)   I only
(B)   II only
(C)   III only
(D)   I and II
(E)   II and III

When you have to decide whether such code is correct, check the boundary conditions first: does it work if we have to insert the element at the very beginning or at the very end of the array? Segment I, for example, looks good at first — very similar to the `InsertInOrder` algorithm described above. But if `newValue` is smaller than all the elements in the array, nothing is inserted. Actually, it is Segment II that is equivalent to the `InsertInOrder` code above, only `for` is replaced with `while` and `if (...) break` is replaced with an additional terminating condition in the `while` loop. Segment III uses a more step-wise approach: first find the place to insert, then shift the elements above that place, then insert. In Segment III it is sufficient to check that this code works for `newValue` being the smallest and the largest — that means there are no tricks. The answer is E.

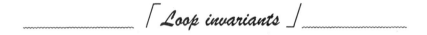

Loop invariants

⌈ AB exam takers should be familiar with the concept of *loop invariants*. A loop invariant is an assertion about the loop that is relevant to the purpose of the loop and that holds true before and after each iteration through the loop. This assertion is usually expressed as a relation between the variables involved in the loop. Loop invariants are used to reason about programs formally and to prove their correctness without tracing all the iterations through a loop. If you can establish that an assertion is true before the first iteration, and also prove that for any iteration if the assertion is true before that iteration it will remain true after that iteration, then your assertion is a loop invariant. If you are familiar with mathematical induction, you can see how it works here. If not, you can still answer questions about loop invariants without too much trouble.

27

Consider the following code segment:

```
int count = 0;
int n = 41;
int k = 2;

while (k <= n)
{
    if (IsPrime(k))
        count++;
    k++;
}
```

Which of the following statements are loop invariants for the above code?

    I.   k is a prime.
   II.   41 is a prime.
  III. count is equal to the number of primes from 2 to k-1.

(A)   I only
(B)   II only
(C)   III only
(D)   I and II
(E)   None of the three

☞ Statement I is not an invariant because it varies: k may or may not be a prime as we iterate through the loop. More precisely, k is a prime before the first iteration (k = 2) and before the second iteration (k = 3), but not after it (k = 4). This eliminates A and D. Statement II is not an invariant for a different reason. Certainly 41 is a prime — so are 37, 43, 47, and an infinite number of other integers. Washington, DC, is also the capital of the United States. These facts, while true, do not help us reason about the purpose or correctness of the above code. But Statement III is a typical invariant: it connects the values of the variables count and k and reflects the purpose of the loop, namely counting all the primes from 2 to n. The answer is C. ↵

3.4. Sequential Search and Binary Search

A typical application of a simple loop is *Sequential Search*:

```
int SequentialSearch(const apvector<int> & A, int n, int target)
// precondition:  Array A holds values A[0], ..., A[n-1].
// postcondition: Returns pos such that 0 <= pos < n and A[pos] == target,
//                   or -1 if target is not among A[0], ..., A[n-1].
{
    int k;

    for (k = 0; k < n; k++)
    {
        if (A[k] == target)
            return k;
    }
    return -1;
}
```

This method works for an array with elements in random order. If an array is sorted (that is, if its elements are arranged in ascending or descending order), then Binary Search is a much more efficient method.

Binary Search is a "divide and conquer" method for quickly finding a target value in a sorted array. Suppose the array is sorted in ascending order. We take the element in the middle (or approximately in the middle) of the array and compare it to the target. If they are equal, we're done. If the target is greater, we continue the search in the right half of the array, and if it's smaller, we continue in the left half. For example:

```
int BinarySearch(const apvector<int> & A, int n, int target)
// precondition:  Array A contains n values sorted in ascending order.
// postcondition: Returns the position of the element equal to target
//                   or -1 if target is not in the array.
{
    int left = 0;
    int right = n - 1;
    int middle;

    while (left <= right)
    {
        middle = (left + right) / 2;
        if (target == A[middle])
            return middle;
        else if (target < A[middle])
            right = middle - 1;    // Continue search in the left half
        else
            left = middle + 1;     // Continue search in the right half
    }
    return -1;
}
```

Binary Search in an array of 2^k - 1 elements requires at most k iterations. In other words, Binary Search in an array of n elements requires $\log_2 n$ iterations. For example, for 1,000,000 elements it needs at most 20 iterations. By comparison, Sequential Search in an array of n elements takes, on average, $n/2$ iterations and, in the worst case, may take n iterations.

28

Suppose a program that uses Binary Search to find a random target value in a sorted array of 30 elements takes, on average, the same time as another program that uses Sequential Search. How much faster, approximately, will the Binary Search program run than the Sequential Search program on an array of 1000 elements?

(A)   2 times faster
(B)   10 times faster
(C)   16 times faster
(D)   33 times faster
(E)   50 times faster

☞ Binary Search takes 5 iterations for 30 elements ($32 = 2^5$) and 10 iterations for 1000 elements ($1024 = 2^{10}$). So Binary Search will run roughly two times longer on a 1000-element array than on a 30-element array. Sequential search will run roughly 33 times longer ($1000 \approx 30 \cdot 33$). On 1000 elements, Binary Search will be $33/2 = 16 \cdot 5$ faster. The answer is C. ☜

29

An e-mail address is a string made of alphanumeric characters, one or several "dots," and one "@." A short substring that follows the last dot is called the domain name suffix. For example, in `jane.lee@math.bestacad.org`, "org" is the suffix. Which of the following methods can be used to find the beginning position of the suffix?

I.   Modified Sequential Search in which we scan through the whole array keeping track of the last occurrence of a given character

II.   Modified Sequential Search which proceeds backwards, starting at end of the array

III.   Modified Binary Search in which each alphanumeric character is treated as '0' and a dot and @ are treated as '1'

(A)   I only
(B)   II only
(C)   III only
(D)   I and II
(E)   II and III

☞ The task is basically to find the last dot in a string. Method I is not the most efficient, but it works:

```
for (k = 0; k < email.length(); k++)
    if (email[k] == '.')
        dotPos = k;
return dotPos;
```

Method II works a bit faster:

```
for (k = email.length() - 1; k >= 0; k--)
    if (email[k] == '.')
        return k;
```

The description of Method III tries to confuse you with binary system which has no relation to Binary Search. The latter won't work here because dots are randomly scattered among alphanumeric characters. The answer is D. ☝

3.5. Selection and Insertion Sorts

Sorting means arranging a list of elements in ascending or descending order, according to the values of the elements or some key that is part of an element. Sorting algorithms are usually discussed for lists represented as arrays. ⌈ In <u>AB exam</u> sorting questions, lists may be represented as linked lists. ⌋

Selection and **Insertion** sorts are called *quadratic sorts* **because they use two straightforward nested loops and the number of required comparisons is approximately proportional to n^2.**

In *Selection Sort* we iterate by k from n down to 2: we find the largest among the first k elements and swap it with the k-th element.

```
void SelectionSort(apvector<int> & A, int n)
// precondition:  Array A contains A[0], ..., A[n-1] (n >= 1)
//                (Assume that the Swap function is coded elsewhere).
// postcondition: Elements are sorted in ascending order.
{
    int i, k, maxPos;

    for (k = n; k >= 2; k--)
    {
        maxPos = 0;
        for (i = 1; i < k; i++)
        {
            if (A[i] > A[maxPos])
                maxPos = i;
        }
        Swap(A[maxPos], A[k-1]);
    }
}
```

In the above function, the inner loop runs k-1 times, for $k = n, n$-1, ..., 2.

The total number of comparisons in Selection Sort is always the same:

$$(n-1)+(n-2)+...+1 = \frac{n(n-1)}{2}$$

In *Insertion Sort*, we iterate for k from 2 up to n. We keep the first $(k$-1$)$ elements sorted and insert the k-th element among them where it belongs:

```
void InsertionSort(apvector<int> & A, int n)
// precondition:  Array A contains A[0], ..., A[n-1] (n >= 1)
// postcondition: Elements are sorted in ascending order.
{
    int i, k;
    int temp;

    for (k = 2; k <= n; k++)
    {
        temp = A[k-1];
        for (i = k-1; i > 0; i--)
        {
            if (A[i-1] <= temp)
                break;
            else
                A[i] = A[i-1];
        }
        A[i] = temp;
    }
}
```

In this version of Insertion Sort, if the array is already sorted, then the inner loop runs just one comparison and we immediately break out of it. Then the function needs a total of n-1 comparisons. This is the best case: instead of *quadratic* time the function executes in *linear* time.

The worst case for this implementation of Insertion Sort is when the array is sorted in reverse order. Then the inner loop runs k-1 times and the whole function will need as many comparisons as Selection Sort:

$$1+2+...+(n-1) = \frac{n(n-1)}{2}$$

The average case is about half of that number, still approximately proportional to n^2.

The functions above are only examples of how Selection and Insertion Sorts can be implemented. Other variations are possible.

|30|

Consider the task of sorting elements of an array in ascending order. Which of the following statements are true?

    I.   Selection Sort always requires more comparisons than Insertion Sort.
   II.   Insertion Sort always requires more moves than Selection Sort.
  III.   Insertion Sort, on average, requires more moves than Selection Sort.

    (A)   I only
    (B)   II only
    (C)   III only
    (D)   I and II
    (E)   II and III

☞ This question gives us a chance to review the properties of the two quadratic sorts. As we have seen, Statement I is false: although, on average, Selection Sort requires more comparisons, Insertion Sort in the worst case (an array sorted in reverse order) will take as many comparisons as Selection Sort. Statement II is false, too: in the best case, when the array is already sorted, Insertion Sort does not require any moves. (Selection Sort, too, with a slight modification, can avoid any moves when the array is already sorted.) Statement III is the vague part: what do we mean, "on average"? First of all, our array must be large enough to make any conclusions. Sorting an array of three elements will not be representative. Let's assume that we set up an experiment where we generate a fairly large array of random numbers, sort it using each of the two algorithms, and count the number of moves. Intuition tells us that Insertion Sort, on average, needs more moves. Indeed, the k-th iteration through the outer loop may require anywhere from 0 to k moves, $k/2$ moves on average. In Selection Sort each iteration through the outer loop requires one swap which can be counted as three moves. The answer is C. ☜

⌈ Insertion Sort works better with a linked list than with an array because inserting an element in the middle of a linked list is easier — you just have to rearrange a few pointers. With a linked list, you can scan the first k-1 elements, starting at the head of the list, and insert the k-th element among them. ⌋

3.6. Recursion

You may find recursion difficult or pleasant, depending on your taste. If you happen to hate it and you are taking the A exam, you can still take a stab at multiple-choice questions on recursion.

31

Consider the following function:

```
void Mystery(int n)
{
    int i;
    if ( n <= 0) return;
    for (i = 0; i < n; i++)
    {
        cout << '-';
    }
    for (i = 0; i < n; i++)
    {
        cout << '+';
    }
    cout << endl;
    Mystery(n-1);               // Recursive call
}
```

What is the output when `Mystery(4)` is called?

(A)
```
----++++
```

(B)
```
-+
-+
-+
-+
```

(C)
```
----+
----++
----+++
----++++
```

(D)
```
-+
--++
---+++
----++++
```

(E)
```
----++++
---+++
--++
-+
```

This function calls itself — that's what recursion is. Note two things about it. First, if n <= 0, the function doesn't do anything. An exit from a recursive function, after some work, perhaps, but without recursive calls, is called the *base case* (or the *stopping case*). In this function the base case does nothing. Second, when the function calls itself, it calls itself with an argument that is less by one than the original. The argument has to change, usually decrease in some way in the direction of the base case, in order for the recursion to terminate at some point.

Instead of trying to unwrap and trace all the recursive calls in this function, first try to reason more formally about its properties. The function prints some minuses followed by the same number of pluses. This eliminates C. The output also cannot be very simple, otherwise what would be the point of recursion? This eliminates A and B. When called with $n = 4$, the function right away prints one line with 4 minuses and 4 pluses. The answer is E. ⏎

Now suppose we change the `Mystery` function in the previous question, placing the recursive call <u>above</u> the `for` loops:

32

Consider the following function:

```
void Mystery(int n)
{
    int i;

    if ( n <= 0) return;
    Mystery(n-1);              // Recursive call
    for (i = 0; i < n; i++)
    {
        cout << '-';
    }
    for (i = 0; i < n; i++)
    {
        cout << '+';
    }
    cout << endl;
}
```

What is the output when `Mystery(4)` is called?

< Same choices as in Question 31 >

☞ This question is a bit trickier, although D and E are still the only plausible answers:

(D)
```
-+
--++
---+++
----++++
```

(E)
```
----++++
---+++
--++
-+
```

We have to choose D because the last thing `Mystery(4)` does is print `----++++`.

(If you are more mathematically inclined, you can reason as follows. `Mystery(4)` prints a triangle pointing either up or down. Let's take a guess at this function's general behavior: say, "`Mystery(n)` prints a triangle with *n* rows that points up." Suppose it's true for *n* = 3. Then `Mystery(4)` first prints a triangle with 3 rows in the recursive call, then adds the longest fourth row. Our guess fits, so the answer should be D.) ✍

33

Consider the following function:

```
void MysteryFun(const apstring & str)
{
    int len = str.length();
    if (len >= 3)
    {
        MysteryFun(str.substr(0, len/3));
        cout << str.substr(len/3, len/3);
        MysteryFun(str.substr(2*len/3, len/3));
    }
}
```

What is the output when `MysteryFun("la-la-la!")` is called?

(A) `la-la-la!`
(B) `ala-a`
(C) `ala-la-la-l`
(D) `lla-l`
(E) `a-la-a!`

✍ Many AP questions mix unrelated subjects. This question tests both recursion and strings and it is a tough question. We start with a string of nine characters, but immediately call `MysteryFun` recursively for a string of three characters. So it makes sense to see first what happens when we call, say, `MysteryFun("xyz")`. This call just prints the middle character, `'y'`, and does nothing else: when `len` is 3 the two recursive calls do nothing. Now back to the original string of nine characters. The two recursive calls print one character each and `cout <<` prints three characters, so the output must have five characters. This eliminates A, C, and E. The first character printed is the middle character in the first 1/3 of the string, which is `'a'`. The answer is B. ✍

_____ *Recursive implementation of Binary Search* _____

The description of the Binary Search algorithm is recursive in nature, and it can be implemented recursively with ease.

34

Consider the following incomplete recursive implementation of Binary Search:

```
int BinarySearch(const apvector<int> & A,
                       int left, int right, int target)
// precondition:  Array A contains values stored from A[left]
//                to A[right], sorted in ascending order.
// postcondition: Returns the position of the element equal to target
//                or -1, if target is not among the values
//                A[left], ..., A[right].
{
    int targetPos = -1;
    int middle;

    < statement 1 >
    {
        middle = (left + right) / 2;
        if (target == A[middle])
            < statement 2 >
        else if (target < A[middle])
            targetPos = BinarySearch(A, left, middle - 1, target);
        else
            targetPos = BinarySearch(A, middle + 1, right, target);
    }
    return targetPos;
}
```

Which of the following could be used to replace < *statement 1* > and < *statement 2* > so that the BinarySearch function works as intended?

	< *statement 1* >	< *statement 2* >
(A)	while (left <= right)	return targetPos;
(B)	while (left <= right)	return middle;
(C)	while (left < right)	targetPos = middle;
(D)	if (left <= right)	targetPos = middle;
(E)	if (left < right)	return middle;

☞ In the choice between while and if, if wins, because this is a <u>recursive</u> solution and recursion replaces iterations. This eliminates A, B, and C. In D and E either choice works for Statement 2, but Statement 1 in E misses the case when left == right. The answer is D. ⏎

AB exams very often include a free-response question on binary trees, so you have to be comfortable with recursive functions that deal with binary trees. Dealing with them in any other way is usually not practical under the time constraints of the exam. Trees are reviewed in Chapter 4.

3.7. Mergesort and Quicksort

Mergesort and *Quicksort* are two recursive sorting algorithms based on the "divide and conquer" principle. Both algorithms take, on average, $n \log n$ comparisons, as opposed to n^2 comparisons in quadratic sorts. This difference can be very significant for large arrays. For example, for 1024 elements, Mergesort and Quicksort may run 100 times faster than Selection Sort and Insertion Sort.

The idea of *Mergesort* is simple: divide the array into two approximately equal halves; sort (recursively) each half, then merge them together into one sorted array (Figure 3-2). Mergesort usually requires a temporary array for holding the two sorted halves before they are merged back into the original space.

Split the array into two halves:

```
A:    1   7   4   9 ┊ 3   5   8   6   2
```

Sort each half (recursively) and copy into *temp*:

```
temp: 1   4   7   9 ┊ 2   3   5   6   8
```

Merge elements in ascending order from the two sorted halves back into the array:

```
temp: 1   4   7   9 ┊ 2   3   5   6   8
A:    1   2   3   _   _   _   _   _   _
```

Figure 3-2. Mergesort

[35]

Consider the following implementation of Mergesort:

```
void Sort(apvector<int> & A, int n1, int n2)
// precondition:  0 <= n1 <= n2 < A.length()
// postcondition: A[n1], ..., A[n2] are sorted in ascending order.
{
    int m;

    if (n1 == n2)
        return;

    m = (n1 + n2) / 2;
    Sort(A, n1, m);
    Sort(A, m+1, n2);
    if (A[m] > A[m+1])        // Optional line
        Merge(A, n1, m, n2);
}
```

Compare it with a more conventional version with the if statement on the "Optional line" removed. Suppose A has 8 elements and Sort(A, 0, 7) is called. For which of the following values in A will the version with if work a bit faster than the version without?

I.   1 2 3 4 5 6 7 8
II. 5 6 7 8 2 1 4 3
III. 2 1 4 3 6 5 8 7

(A)   I only
(B)   I and II
(C)   I and III
(D)   I, II, and III
(E)   None of the three

A typical implementation of Mergesort doesn't skip the work even when the array is already sorted. The slight change proposed in this question allows Mergesort to skip all the merging and quickly establish that an array is already sorted, as in Array I. This version also avoids merging when the array is partially sorted, namely when all the values in the left half of the array are smaller than any value in the right half, as in Array III. In that case, after the two recursive calls to Sort the array becomes sorted and the call to Merge is skipped.

Since the algorithm is recursive, it will also save time when some portions of the array have these properties — are either sorted or partially sorted — even when the whole array isn't. In Array II, for example, the left half is sorted and the right half is partially sorted. The answer is D.

Quicksort is a little less obvious. It works as follows. Choose a "pivot" element. Rearrange all the elements of the array so that the pivot divides the array into two parts. All the elements to the left of the pivot should be less or equal to the pivot. All the elements to the right of the pivot should be greater or equal to the pivot. Sort (recursively) each part.

Quicksort does not require temporary storage. On average, it runs a bit faster than Mergesort, but it is less predictable. We have to be lucky when we choose a pivot; hopefully its value is close to the median value for the array, so that the pivot divides the array into two roughly equal halves.

36

The function

```
QuickSort(apvector<int> & A, int k, int m);
```

implements the recursive Quicksort algorithm that sorts the elements A[k], ... A[m] in ascending order. It is implemented in such a way that A[k] serves as the pivot element. Which of the following ordering properties of the array A with 1000 elements results in the best running time for QuickSort(A, 0, 999)?

(A)   When A[0], ..., A[999] are already sorted in ascending order
(B)   When A[0], ..., A[999] are sorted in descending order
(C)   When A[0] is the median of A[0], ..., A[999] and the rest of the 999 elements are sorted in ascending order
(D)   When A[999] is the median of A[0], ..., A[999] and the rest of the 999 elements are sorted in ascending order
(E)   When A[0], ..., A[999] are arranged in random order

☞ Quicksort is a recursive algorithm, which means that the function will be called many times for different segments of the array. For it to run efficiently, the pivot element in these calls must pretty often be close to the median value of the segment. When the array is already sorted, as in A and B, the first element, which is chosen as pivot, is always as far from the median as possible. In such situations the pivot does not split the array into two more or less equal halves; instead it just splits away one element. So these two are the worst cases for Quicksort. In C and D the first element is the median, but this applies only at the top level of recursion. As we proceed deeper with recursive calls, the smaller segments become sorted and we face the same problem as in A and B. The random arrangement ensures that with some frequency the first element will be somewhat close to the median and QuickSort will work as intended. The answer is E. ☚

3.8. "Best Design" Questions

A typical AP exam may contain one or two such questions. Here are two examples:

37

Consider designing a data structure that represents information about subscribers in an e-mail server system using the following structure:

```
struct Subscriber
{
    int subscriberID;
    int numMessages;
};
```

Information about all subscribers who have unread mail will be stored in an array with elements of the type Subscriber. Two possible implementations are being considered:

Method A: Store the array entries in arbitrary order.
Method B: Store the array entries in sorted order by subscriber ID.

Consider the following operations:

Operation 1:   Increment the number of messages for a specified subscriber in the array.
Operation 2:   Add a new subscriber with a given number of messages to the list of subscribers.

Which of the following is true?

(A)   Both Operation 1 and Operation 2 can be implemented more efficiently using Method A than Method B.
(B)   Both Operation 1 and Operation 2 can be implemented more efficiently using Method B than Method A.
(C)   Operation 1 can be implemented more efficiently using Method A; Operation 2 can be implemented more efficiently using Method B.
(D)   Operation 1 can be implemented more efficiently using Method B; Operation 2 can be implemented more efficiently using Method A.
(E)   Operation 1 and Operation 2 can be implemented equally efficiently using either method.

☞ These types of questions may test your reading comprehension skills, but in terms of real technical difficulty they don't go too far beyond common sense. It certainly helps if you have a good understanding of various data structures and their uses in different algorithms. Here, for example, we have to deal with finding an element with a given key (subscriber ID) in an array and inserting a new element into an array. The relevant ideas that come to mind are Sequential and Binary Search, inserting an element in order, and inserting at the end.

You may want to jot down a little table quickly in order not to get confused in the Methods and Operations and then check the appropriate boxes (that work faster):

	A: random order	B: sorted
1. Increment # msgs — "find"		✓
2. Add a subscr — "insert".	✓	

Clearly, if you need to worry about the order, adding a subscriber to the sorted array will take more work than just slapping him on at the end. This alone eliminates choices B, C, and E. (Don't try to be too smart, thinking that you may need to reallocate, resize, and copy the array if it is not large enough. This is not what this question is about.)

Is it easier to find a value in a sorted array? Of course. If you remember that you can use Binary Search in a sorted array, that's great. But even if you don't, this would be a good guess. The fact that the array is sorted probably can't hurt the search operation. This eliminates A. The answer is D.

Questions 38-39 refer to the following information:

The College Board administers AP exams in N subjects ($N \geq 38$) over K days ($K \geq 14$). Each subject is offered only on one day. The subjects are represented by integers from 1 to N. Two different designs are being considered for an application that keeps track of the exam calendar:

Design 1:

The exam schedule information is held in a one-dimensional array of integers. For each of the K days there is one entry that represents the number of exams on that day, followed by the list of the subjects offered on that day. For example, if the first day has two exams in subjects 29 and 38, and the second day has no exams, the array will start with 2, 29, 38, 0, ...

Design 2:

The schedule is represented as a two-dimensional array of size N by K. The elements of the array are Boolean values: `true` indicates that the given subject is offered on a given day.

38

Assuming that integers are represented using four bytes and Boolean values using one byte, which of the following statements about the space requirements of the two designs is true?

(A)   Design 1 will require less space.
(B)   Design 2 will require less space.
(C)   Which design will require more space depends on the value of N.
(D)   Which design will require more space depends on the value of K.
(E)   Which design will require more space depends on the number of bytes it takes to represent Boolean and integer values in the computer memory.

 See the solution for Question 39

39

Suppose that Design 2 is chosen and that the following function is implemented as efficiently as possible:

Given a subject number between 1 and N and a day number between 1 and K, the function returns `true` if the given subject is offered on the given day, and `false` otherwise.

Which of the following statements is true?

(A)   The average time spent in the function is proportional to N.
(B)   The average time spent in the function is proportional to K.
(C)   The average time spent in the function is proportional to the total number of elements in the array (N times K).
(D)   The average time spent in the function is proportional to the average number of exams per day.
(E)   The time spent in the function does not depend on N or K, nor on the distribution of exams by day.

👉 👉 The above two questions compare space and time requirements for the same data represented as a list (Design 1) and as a two-dimensional *lookup table* (Design 2). You can answer these questions right away if you are familiar with lookup tables. In a lookup table, a data item (here a valid subject/day pair) is represented as a <u>location</u> in an array (here, row/col). Lookup tables usually take more space but provide instantaneous (constant time) access to data regardless of the size of the table.

If you've never heard the term *lookup table*, you can still figure it out.

In Question 38 the space requirement for Design 1 is $K + N$ integers: one for each day (representing the number of exams for that day) and one for each exam (each exam has to be listed under one of the days). The space requirement for Design 2 is $N \cdot K$ Boolean values. $4 \cdot (K + N) < N \cdot K$ for large enough N and K (recall that $N \geq 38$, $K \geq 14$). The answer is A. 👈

In Question 39, you must know that you can go directly to any element of a matrix, `table[d][e]` (or, perhaps, `table[d-1][e-1]` if days and subjects are counted starting from 1 and subscripts start from 0, as in C++.) This property is called *random access* and that's what arrays are all about. The answer is E. 👈

Chapter 4. AB Exam Topics: Linked Lists, Stacks, Queues, Trees, etc.

⌈ All the material in this chapter is needed only for the <u>AB exam</u>. ⌋

4.1. Linked Lists

The nodes of a linked list are scattered in memory, but each node contains a pointer to the next node. A pointer to the first node identifies the list. In the last node of the list, the pointer is set to NULL.

A node of a linked list is usually represented as a structure. For example:

```
struct Node
{
    apstring info;
    Node * next;
};
```

Node, info and next are not reserved words — they are names given by a programmer (or by an exam developer). So instead of Node we may have, for example, ClubMember. A node may have several data elements of different types, not necessarily one apstring.

Usually, nodes of a linked list are dynamically allocated using the new operator, and all nodes and their elements are accessed through pointers.

For example:

```
Node * p;
...
p = new Node;
p->info = str;
p->next = NULL;
```

The Node structure may have a constructor with an initializer list that sets its elements to specified values.

For example:

```
struct Node
{
    apstring info;
    Node * next;

    Node (const apstring & someInfo, Node * somePtr);    // Constructor
};

// Implementation:

Node::Node(const apstring & someInfo, Node * somePtr)
  : info(someInfo), next(somePtr)
{}
```

In this version you have to allocate and initialize a Node object in the same statement. For example:

```
Node * p;
...
p = new Node(str, NULL);
```

_____ *Linked list traversals* _____

You can use a for loop to conveniently traverse a linked list. Suppose a pointer head points to the first node in the list. Then you can write:

```
Node * p;
for (p = head; p != NULL; p = p->next)
{
    cout << p->info << endl;   // ... or do whatever processing
                               //      is required
}
```

Sequential Search in a linked list may be implemented, for example, as follows:

```
Node * SequentialSearch(Node * head, const apstring & target)
// precondition:  head points to a linked list.
// postcondition: Returns a pointer to the first node that contains target
//                or NULL if not found.
{
    Node * p;

    for (p = head; p != NULL; p = p->next)
    {
        if (p->info == target)
            break;
    }
    return p;
}
```

Another variation uses a `while` loop with a return directly from the loop:

```
Node * SequentialSearch(Node * head, const apstring & target)
// precondition:  head points to a linked list.
// postcondition: Returns a pointer to the first node that contains target
//                or NULL if not found.
{
    Node * p = head;

    while (p != NULL)
    {
        if (p->info == target)
            return p;
        p = p->next;
    }
    return NULL;
}
```

Insert function

The `Insert` function below adds a new node <u>at the front</u> of a list. This implementation assumes that `Node` has a constructor with two arguments, as mentioned above. The `head` pointer is passed to `Insert` <u>by reference</u> because the function changes it.

```
void Insert(Node * & head, const apstring & str)
// precondition:  head points to a linked list.
// postcondition: A node, containing str is inserted at the
//                front of the list.
{
    Node * p = new Node(str, head);
    head = p;
}
```

New nodes are never declared as variables; only <u>pointers</u> to nodes are declared and the nodes are dynamically allocated using the `new` operator.

```
...                              ...
Node newNode(str, head);         Node * newNode = new Node(str, head);
// Never used                     // Ok! newNode here is a pointer
```

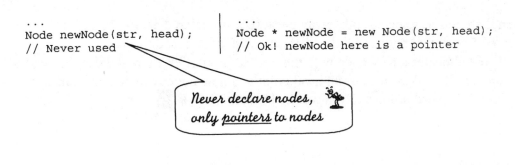

Never declare nodes, only <u>pointers</u> to nodes

Questions 40-41 refer to the following definitions:

```
struct Student
{
    apstring name;
    double GPA;
    Student * next;

    Student (const apstring & nm, double gp, Student * nx);
};

Student::Student (const apstring & nm, double gp, Student * nx)
  : name(nm), GPA(gp), next(nx)
{}


Student * studentList;
```

40

Assuming that `studentList` points to a list of students, which of the following code segments correctly allocates a new node for a student with the name "Lobatschewsky" and GPA 3.7, and appends it at the head of the list?

    I.
```
Student x("Lobatschewsky", 3.7, studentList);
studentList = x;
```

    II.
```
Student * x = new Student("Lobatschewsky", 3.7, studentList);
studentList = x;
```

    III.
```
studentList = new Student("Lobatschewsky", 3.7, studentList);
```

(A)   I only
(B)   II only
(C)   III only
(D)   I and II
(E)   II and III

☞ Segment I should be rejected right away because x is declared as `Student`, not `Student *`. Recall that nodes of linked lists are always accessed through pointers. Segment II first allocates a new node with the desired properties, then updates the head of the list. Segment III makes the current head point to a new node, which is initialized to the old value of the head pointer. Both work. The answer is E. ↵

41

Consider a function that appends a node at the tail of a list of students:

```
void InsertAtTail(Student * & studentList,
                         const apstring & nm, double gp)
// precondition:  studentList is NULL or points to a list of students.
// postcondition: A new node with given information is added
//                at the tail of the list.
{
    Student * tail = studentList;
    < code >
}
```

Which of the following code segments may be substituted for < *code* > so that the function `InsertAtTail` works as intended?

```
I.    if (studentList == NULL)
      {
          studentList = new Student(nm, gp, NULL);
      }
      else
      {
          while (tail->next != NULL)
              tail = tail->next;
          tail = new Student(nm, gp, NULL);
      }
```

```
II.   while (tail != NULL && tail->next != NULL)
          tail = tail->next;
      if (tail == NULL)
          studentList = new Student(nm, gp, NULL);
      else
          tail->next = new Student(nm, gp, NULL);
```

```
III.  Student * newNode = new Student(nm, gp, NULL);
      if (tail != NULL)
      {
          while (tail->next != NULL)
              tail = tail->next;
          tail->next = newNode;
      }
      else
      {
          studentList = newNode;
      }
```

(A)   I only
(B)   II only
(C)   III only
(D)   I and II
(E)   II and III

☞ This is too much code for a typical multiple-choice question, but we can find some clues in it quickly.

Segment I may look straightforward at first, but the last line has a bug: it sets `tail`, a local variable, to `newNode`, instead of saving `newNode` in `tail->next`, that is, in the `next` pointer in the last node of the original list.

In Segment II, the condition

```
(tail != NULL && tail->next != NULL)
```

may look suspicious at first, but it works due to short-circuit evaluation. If `studentList` is empty at the beginning, then `tail` is `NULL` and the `while` loop is not executed. Otherwise `tail` advances until it points to the last node of the list. The following `if-else` statement correctly sets either `tail->next` or `studentList` to the new node. So, Segment II works.

Segment III takes a step-wise approach: it first allocates and sets values in a new node, then appends it to the list. It works, and, in fact, this approach may be cleaner. The answer is, again, E. ☜

4.2. Stacks and Queues, the `apstack` and `apqueue` Classes

The Stack ADT (abstract data type) is a storage structure that implements the last-in-first-out (LIFO) storage method. A stack is controlled by two operations: *push* places an element on the top of the stack and *pop* removes and returns the top element. Stacks are used for untangling hierarchical nested structures and branching processes.

In AP materials, stacks are always implemented using the templated `apstack` class.

For example:

```
apstack<int> s;            // Declare an empty stack of integers
apstack<int> s2 = s;       // Declare another stack and copy s into it
apstack<int> s3(s2);       // The same as: apstack<int> s3 = s2;
```

`apstack` arguments are always passed to functions by reference. They are normally not `const` because if a stack doesn't change, what's the point of using it?

The following function removes all the elements from a stack of `doubles` and pushes those that are positive on another stack:

```
int RestackPositives(apstack<double> & s1, apstack<double> & s2)
// precondition:  s1 holds several elements or is empty; s2 is empty.
// postcondition: s2 holds all positive elements from s1 in reverse order;
//                s1 is empty.  Returns the number of elements on s2.
//
{
    double x;

    while (!s1.isEmpty())
    {
        s1.pop(x);
        if (x > 0)
            s2.push(x);
    }
    return s2.length();
}
```

42

Assume that s1 and s2 are of the type apstack<char> and contain the following values:

Consider the following code segment:

```
apstack<char> s3;
char ch;
while (!s1.isEmpty() && !s2.isEmpty())
{
    s1.pop(ch);
    s3.push(ch);
    s2.pop(ch);
    s3.push(ch);
    s1.push(ch);
}
```

Which of the following best represents s3 after the code segment executes?

```
                              top
                               ↓
(A)    i e h r e e r h e t
(B)    h t t h h e e r r e
(C)    i e e r r e e h h t
(D)    e i r e e r h e t h
(E)                i e h r
```

☞ This question is not as difficult as it might seem. Since the first character that is pushed onto s3 comes from the top of s1, it is 'i'. The second comes from the top of s2; it is 'e'. 'e' is also pushed back onto s1, so the third character, which again comes from the top of s1, is 'e' again. Therefore, the characters at the bottom of s3 must be "iee." The answer is C. ☜

Other apstack functions

Besides push, pop, isEmpty, and length, the apstack class has a couple of other functions:

```
itemType & top();      // Returns the top element without popping
                       //   it from the stack
void pop();            // This overloaded version pops the top element
                       //   and discards it
void makeEmpty();      // Empties the stack
```

It also has an overloaded assignment operator, so if you write

```
s2 = s;
```

the whole stack s is copied into s2.

Queues

The Queue ADT is a storage structure that implements the first-in-first-out (FIFO) storage method. A queue is controlled by two operations: *enqueue* places an element at the end of the queue and *dequeue* removes and returns the front element. Queues are used for processing events in the order of their arrival.

In AP materials, queues are always implemented using the templated apqueue class.

For example:

```
apqueue<char> q;         // Declare an empty queue of chars
apqueue<char> q2 = q;    // Declare another queue and copy q into it
apqueue<char> q3(q2);    // The same as: apqueue<char> q3 = q2;
```

apqueue arguments are always passed to functions by reference, and they are normally not const.

The following function reads lines from an open text file, puts all "#include" lines into a queue, and returns the number of lines queued:

```
int ExtractIncludeLines(istream & inFile, apqueue<apstring> & q)
// precondition:  inFile is a text file open for reading.
// postcondition: All lines from inFile that begin with #include
//                are inserted into q.  Returns the number of lines queued.
{
    apstring line;

    while (getline(inFile, line))
    {
        if (line.substr(0, 8) == "#include")
            q.enqueue(line);
    }
    return q.length();
}
```

```
43
```

Consider the following function:

```
void Parse(const apstring & exp)
{
    int j, k;
    apstack<int> s;
    apqueue<apstring> q;
    apstring str;

    for (k = 0; k < exp.length(); k++)
    {
        if (exp[k] == '(' )
        {
            s.push(k);
        }
        else if (exp[k] == ')' )
        {
            if (s.isEmpty())
            {
                cout << "*** Syntax error ***" << endl;
                return;
            }
            s.pop(j);
            q.enqueue(exp.substr(j+1, k-j-1));
        }
    }

    if (!s.isEmpty())
    {
        cout << "*** Syntax error ***" << endl;
    }
    else
    {
        while (!q.isEmpty())
        {
            q.dequeue(str);
            cout << str << endl;
        }
    }
}
```

What is the output when `Parse("Evaluate(((a+b)*(a-b))/2)")` is called?

(A)
```
a+b
a-b
(a+b)*(a-b)
((a+b)*(a-b))/2
```

(B)
```
Evaluate(((a+b)*(a-b))/2)
((a+b)*(a-b))/2
(a+b)*(a-b)
a+b
a-b
```

(C)
```
((a+b)*(a-b))/2
(a+b)*(a-b)
a+b
a-b
```

(D)
```
a+b
a-b
```

(E)
```
*** Syntax error ***
```

☞ This example is a bit too long. Indeed, something like this would probably be more appropriate for part of a free-response question. In this function a stack is used to untangle an expression with nested parentheses and a queue is used for storing extracted parenthesized subexpressions when they are found. This is a reasonable example of what stacks and queues might be used for. As soon as an opening parenthesis is found, its position is saved on the stack; when a closing parenthesis is found, the saved opening position is popped from the stack and the substring between them (excluding the parentheses themselves) is added to the queue. The use of a stack automatically assures that the opening and closing parentheses for a substring are indeed a matching pair. The stack must be empty at the end, otherwise a syntax error is reported because the parentheses do not match. In this example, `exp` is `"Evaluate(((a+b)*(a-b))/2)"`. The parentheses do match, so E is not the right answer. Their contents is printed for each pair of matching parentheses, so D is not the right answer either. There are four matching pairs, so the output must contain exactly four lines, as in A and C. The inner expressions end up closer to the top of the stack, so they will be queued and printed first. The answer is A. ☜

----------- *Other apqueue functions* -----------

Besides enqueue, dequeue, isEmpty, and length, the apqueue class has a couple of other functions:

```
itemType & front();   // Returns the first element without removing
                       //   it from the queue
void dequeue();        // This overloaded version removes the front element
                       //   and discards it
void makeEmpty();      // Empties the queue
```

It also has an overloaded assignment operator, so if you write

```
q2 = q;
```

the whole queue q is copied into q2.

4.3. Binary Trees

In a binary tree, each node, except the *root*, has one parent. Each node contains pointers to its left and right children; a NULL value indicates that the corresponding child is not in the tree. A node that doesn't have any children is called a *leaf*. Each node is a root of a smaller binary tree, its *subtree* (Figure 4-1).

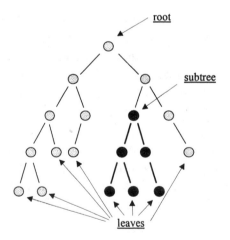

Figure 4-1.   Binary tree

A node of a binary tree may be represented by the following structure with a constructor:

```
struct TreeNode
{
    apstring info;
    TreeNode * left;
    TreeNode * right;

    TreeNode(const apstring & str, TreeNode * lt, TreeNode * rt);
};

TreeNode::TreeNode(const apstring & str, TreeNode * lt, TreeNode * rt)
    : info(str), left(lt), right(rt)
{}
```

Nodes of a tree are usually dynamically allocated and always addressed through pointers. A pointer, often called `root`, points to the root node and identifies the tree. A NULL value of the `root` pointer indicates that the tree is empty.

Trees are almost always handled recursively. Recursive code for trees doesn't use any loops.

Recursion can be readily applied because a tree is an inherently recursive structure: the subtree that grows from each node is a smaller binary tree. Recursive code is usually much more compact and readable. The following function, for example, returns the total number of nodes in a tree:

```
int NodeCount(TreeNode * T)
// precondition:  T points to the root node of a binary tree.
// postcondition: Returns the number of nodes in the tree.
{
    if (T == NULL)        // Base case: empty tree
        return 0;
    else                  // Recursive case: 1 for the root plus
                          //    count in left and right subtrees
        return 1 + NodeCount(T->left) + NodeCount(T->right);
}
```

Tree traversals

A process of visiting (e.g., printing the information in) each node of a tree is called *traversal*. The three common types of binary tree traversals are *inorder*, *preorder*, and *postorder*:

```
void TraverseInorder(TreeNode * T)
{
    if (T != NULL)
    {
        TraverseInorder(T->left);
        cout << T->info << endl;        // Visit root in the middle
        TraverseInorder(T->right);
    }
}

void TraversePreorder(TreeNode * T)
{
    if (T != NULL)
    {
        cout << T->info << endl;        // Visit root first
        TraversePreorder(T->left);
        TraversePreorder(T->right);
    }
}

void TraversePostorder(TreeNode * T)
{
    if (T != NULL)
    {
        TraversePostorder(T->left);
        TraversePostorder(T->right);
        cout << T->info << endl;        // Visit root last
    }
}
```

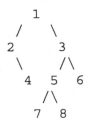

Consider the following binary tree:

```
        1
      /   \
     2     3
      \    /\
       4  5  6
       /\
      7  8
```

Which of the following sequences describes the preorder traversal of this tree?

(A)   1 2 3 4 5 6 7 8
(B)   1 2 4 3 5 7 8 6
(C)   1 4 2 3 5 6 7 8
(D)   4 2 1 3 6 5 8 7
(E)   2 4 1 7 5 8 3 6

☞ In preorder traversal we visit the root first, then the left subtree, and then the right subtree. So the correct sequence should begin with 1, followed by 2, and it should end with 6. The answer is B. ☜

Questions 45-46 assume that a node of a binary tree is represented by the following structure:

```
struct TreeNode
{
    apstring info;
    TreeNode * left;
    TreeNode * right;
};
```

45

Consider an incomplete implementation of the following function:

```
void TotalPaths(TreeNode * T, const apstring & target,
        int & count, int & lengthSum)
// precondition:  T points to the root of a binary tree.
// postcondition: count is set to the total number of
//                nodes in the tree that match target and
//                lengthSum is set to the sum of the lengths of paths
//                that lead from the root to such nodes.
{
    int count1, count2;
    int lengthSum1, lengthSum2;

    if (T == NULL)
    {
        count = 0;
        lengthSum = 0;
        return;
    }
    TotalPaths(T->left, target, count1, lengthSum1);
    TotalPaths(T->right, target, count2, lengthSum2);
    < Missing code >
}
```

Which of the following code segments completes the function so that it works as intended?

I.
```
count = count1 + count2;
if (T->info == target)
    count++;
lengthSum = lengthSum1 + lengthSum2 + 2;
```

II.
```
count = count1 + count2;
if (T->info == target)
    count++;
lengthSum = lengthSum1 + lengthSum2 + count1 +
count2;
```

III.
```
count = 0;
lengthSum = 0;
if (count1 > 0)
{
    count += count1;
    lengthSum += (lengthSum1 + count1);
}
if (count2 > 0)
{
    count += count2;
    lengthSum += (lengthSum2 + count2);
}
if (T->info == target)
    count++;
```

(A)   I only
(B)   II only
(C)   III only
(D)   I and II
(E)   II and III

☞ You might be asked to write something like the `TotalPaths` function in the free-response section of the exam, too. Segment I should be rejected because it adds 2 to `lengthSum` whether or not any matching nodes are found in the subtrees; it fails, for instance, if the tree has just one node. This eliminates A and D. It is possible to verify formally that Segments II and III give the same result. Indeed, after a call to `TotalPaths`, if `count` is 0 then `lengthSum` is 0, too. Therefore, the `if (count... > 0)` statements in Segment II are redundant. The answer is E. ↵

In this function, the values returned from the recursive step have to be adjusted in order for them to work for the top level. We find the sum of the lengths of all paths that start in `root->left`, but now these paths have to be extended to the root. So we have to add 1 to the length of each path, and we can achieve that by adding `count1` to `lengthSum1`. We do the same, of course, for the right subtree. Hence

```
lengthSum = lengthSum1 + lengthSum2 + count1 + count2;
```

46

Consider the following incomplete implementation of a function `IsEqual` that compares two trees:

```
bool IsEqual (TreeNode * T1, TreeNode * T2)
// postcondition:  Returns true if the trees pointed to by T1
//                  and T2 have the same shape and contain.
//                  the same information in the corresponding nodes,
//                  false otherwise.
{
    if (T1 == NULL && T2 == NULL)
        return true;
    else if (T1 == NULL || T2 == NULL)
        return false;
    else
    {
        return < expression >;
    }
}
```

Consider the following two replacements for < *expression* > :

I. "Preorder":

```
T1->info == T2->info &&
IsEqual(T1->left, T2->left) &&
IsEqual(T1->right, T2->right)
```

II. "Postorder":

```
IsEqual(T1->left, T2->left) &&
IsEqual(T1->right, T2->right) &&
T1->info == T2->info
```

Suppose T1 and T2 point to the following trees:

How many times will the operator `==` for `apstrings` execute in each of the two implementations when `IsEqual(T1, T2)` is called?

	Preorder	Postorder
(A)	1	0
(B)	3	2
(C)	3	1
(D)	4	1
(E)	4	4

☞ This is not an easy question because you have to approach it in just the right way. Also you have to keep in mind short-circuit evaluation. The preorder implementation compares all nodes in corresponding places, starting at the root, then the left subtree and right subtree, and proceeds for as long as they match. So it will verify the match for "Atlanta," "Boston," "Cincinnati," and "Denver." This eliminates A, B, and C. In the postorder implementation we compare only the nodes in corresponding places whose left and right subtrees match. There is only one such node here, "Boston" (a leaf). The answer is D. ☙

Binary Search Trees

Binary Search Trees (BSTs) are structures that organize information for fast searching. They implement very directly the "divide-and-conquer" method, similar to Binary Search in sorted arrays, but they also allow relatively fast insertions and removals of elements (the time is roughly proportional to log n, where n is the total number of nodes). The nodes of a BST contain elements for which an order relation (less than, greater than, etc.) is established: they can be numbers, strings, or structures containing some keys that can be compared. Usually all nodes contain different values.

The following property is the defining property of a BST: each node is greater than all the nodes in its left subtree and less than all the nodes in its right subtree.

This property guarantees a simple and quick search method:

```
TreeNode * Find(TreeNode * root, const apstring & target)
// precondition:  root points to a BST.
// postcondition: Returns a pointer to the node that contains target,
//                or NULL if target is not in the tree.
{
    if (root == NULL || target == root->info)
        return root;
    else if (target < root->info)
        return Find(root->left, target);
    else // if (target > root->info)
        return Find(root->right, target);
}
```

Inorder traversal of a BST produces the sequence of its nodes in ascending order. BSTs cannot have multiple nodes with the same value.

47

A binary search tree is built by inserting the following values in this sequence:

'F' 'L' 'O' 'R' 'I' 'D' 'A'

The nodes are appended as leaves in the appropriate places as determined by their alphabetical ordering. Which of the following sequences corresponds to the preorder traversal of the resulting binary search tree?

(A)   F L O R I D A
(B)   A D F I L O R
(C)   F D A L I O R
(D)   R O L I F D A
(E)   I D A F O L R

 Since 'F' is inserted first, it becomes the root and it will be the first in preorder traversal. This eliminates B, D, and E. Choice A would work if it were a queue, not a binary search tree. The answer is C.

Note that if you were asked to arrange the letters "FLORIDA" into a binary search tree with the smallest possible number of levels —

```
        I
       / \
      D   O
     /\   /\
    A  F L  R
```

— then the answer would be E.

The average search time in a BST is approximately proportional to the average length of a path from the root to a node.

If a BST tree is "bushy," with all its levels almost filled with nodes, the search time is roughly proportional to log n (where n is the number of nodes). But in the worst case, when a tree deteriorates into an almost linear structure, with only a few nodes in each level, then the search time may become proportional to n.

4.4. Heaps and Priority Queues, Heapsort

The Priority Queue ADT (abstract data type) is a structure for handling events in order of their priority or rank. Events with the same priority must be handled in a FIFO (first-in-first-out) manner. Suppose an event is represented as a structure:

```
struct Event
{
    apstring info;
    int priority;
    int arrivalTime;
};
```

Then two events may be compared based on their priorities and arrival times. For example, we can use the overloaded > operator to compare events:

```
bool operator > (const Event & event1, const Event & event2)
// postcondition: Returns true if event1 must be processed first,
//                false otherwise.
{
    return (event1.priority > event2.priority) ||
           (event1.priority == event2.priority &&
                              event1.arrivalTime < event2.arrivalTime);
}
```

Then `event1 > event2` means `event1` must be processed first.

A convenient method for implementing priority queues is a particular type of binary tree called a *heap*.

A heap is a binary tree with two additional properties:

1. Completeness — each level, except perhaps the bottom one, is filled with nodes. The last level may have nodes missing on the right side.

2. Ordering — each node is greater than or equal to all the nodes in its left and right subtrees.

For example:

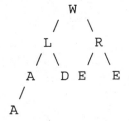

It is easy to find the largest node in a heap — it is its root.

The completeness property allows us to store a heap in an array. The nodes are simply stored in order of scanning all levels top to bottom, left to right. In C++ implementations, it is convenient to leave the first element of the array unused, because in algorithms that handle heaps it is easier to have the root of the heap in the element of the array with subscript 1. The above tree, for example may be stored as

```
<empty> W L R A D E E A
```

In this scheme, a[1] is the root. If a[i] is a node, its parent is found in a[i/2] and its left and right children, if present, are found in a[2*i] and a[2*i+1].

It is not required that all the nodes of a heap be different; but if a heap represents a priority queue, all its nodes will differ, presumably, at least in the order of their arrival.

Nodes are always removed from a heap from its root.

After the root is removed, the heap is repaired by moving its last leaf (that is, the rightmost node in the bottom row) to the root and then "reheaping it down" until the ordering property is restored. "Reheaping down" is swapping the node that is out of order with its largest child until it falls into place.

A node is inserted by adding it as a new leaf to the bottom row, then "reheaping it up" until the ordering is restored. "Reheaping up" is swapping the node that is out of order with its parent until it falls into place.

The time of both removal and insertion operations, on average as well as in the worst case, is roughly proportional to log *n*, where *n* is the number of nodes.

Questions 48-49 refer to the following class that represents a heap of integers. The heap is stored in the apvector myElements with the first element unused:

```
class Heap
{
  public:
    Heap(int len);              // Constructor
    void Insert(int x);
    int Remove();
    < other public member functions >

  private:
    int myNumElements;
    apvector<int> myElements;   // myElements[0] is not used
    < other private members >
};

Heap::Heap(int len)
  : myNumElements(0), myElements(len+1)
{}
```

48

Consider the following function:

```
int Heap::LargestChild(int i)
// precondition:  1 <= i <= myNumElements
// postcondition: Returns the node number for the largest child of i
//                or 0 if node i is a leaf.
{
    if (i > myNumElements/2)
        return 0;
    < code >
    return i;
}
```

Which of the following statement(s) could replace < *code* > so that this function works as specified?

(A)   if (i < myNumElements && myElements[i] < myElements[i+1]) i++;
(B)   if (i < myNumElements - 1 && myElements[i] < myElements[i+1]) i++;
(C)   i *= 2; if (i < myNumElements - 1 && myElements[i] < myElements[i+1]) i--;
(D)   i *= 2; if (i < myNumElements && myElements[i] < myElements[i+1]) i++;
(E)   if (i < myNumElements / 2 && myElements[2*i] < myElements[2*i+1]) i *= 2;

☞ In this implementation of a heap, nodes are numbered from 1 to myNumElements. Recall that in this scheme the children of the node i are numbered 2*i and 2*i+1. The answer is D. ☟

49

Consider the following incomplete implementation of the `Insert` member function that adds an element to the heap:

```
void Heap::Insert(int x)
// precondition:  myNumElements + 1 < myElements.length()
{
    int i, iPar;

    myNumElements++;
    i = myNumElements;
    iPar = i/2;

    while ( < condition > )
    {
        < statement >
        i = iPar;
        iPar = i/2;
    }

    myElements[iPar] = x;
}
```

Which of the following could be used to replace < *condition* > and < *statement* > so that the function `Insert` works as intended?

	< *condition* >	< *statement* >
(A)	`i > 1 && myElements[iPar] > x`	`myElements[i] = myElements[iPar];`
(B)	`iPar > 1 && myElements[iPar] < x`	`myElements[i] = myElements[iPar];`
(C)	`i > 1 && myElements[iPar] > x`	`myElements[iPar] = myElements[i];`
(D)	`iPar > 1 && myElements[iPar] < x`	`myElements[iPar] = myElements[i];`
(E)	`i > 1 && myElements[iPar] < x`	`myElements[i] = x;`

☞ This function implements the "reheap up" algorithm. First we increment `myNumElements` to create a vacancy at the end of the heap. Then we keep moving the parent node down for as long as it remains smaller than x, or until we reach the root of the heap. That moves the vacancy up the heap, until we reach the right place to insert x. Note that before the `while` loop `myElements[i]` is vacant. It has to be filled at the first iteration, so the < *statement* > in C and D won't work. E won't work either, because it doesn't make sense to insert x multiple times. Choice A has to be rejected for two reasons. First, after the `while` loop, i is 1, so iPar is 0. We place x into `myElements[iPar]`, but we know that `myElements[0]` is not used. Second, the comparison with x is backwards. The answer is B. ↵

_____ *Heapsort* _____

Another application of heaps is *Heapsort*.

| **Heapsort is an $n \log n$ sorting method that does not require additional space.**

Suppose we have a list of elements. In the first phase of the Heapsort we can start with an empty heap and insert all the elements from the list into it. In the second phase we remove the elements one by one from the top of the heap and store them back into the list in reverse order. We will end up with a list sorted in ascending order.

If a list is stored in an array, there is an efficient algorithm that reorders its elements in the same place in such a way that the array becomes a representation of a heap. We then remove the elements from the top of this heap and store them starting at the end of the same array in reverse order. This algorithm eliminates the need for additional workspace.

50

Suppose Heapsort is used to sort an array of nine elements in ascending order in the same place without additional work space. The first phase of the algorithm rearranges the elements of the array to form a heap. At the second phase the elements are removed one-by-one from the top of the heap and placed in order starting at the end of the array. Suppose the following sequence represents a heap built after the first phase of Heapsort:

    9 6 8 3 4 7 5 2 1

Which of the following sequences may represent the elements of the array after two iterations through the second phase of Heapsort?

(A)   6 3 4 7 5 2 1 8 9
(B)   7 5 1 2 6 3 4 8 9
(C)   8 9 6 3 4 7 5 2 1
(D)   9 6 8 5 4 7 1 2 3
(E)   7 6 5 3 4 1 2 8 9

☞ After two iterations, the two largest elements, 9 and 8, must be in place at the end of the array. This eliminates C and D. The next largest element, 7, must be at the top of the heap, that is, at the beginning of the array. This eliminates A. To decide between B and E we have to find out which one represents a heap in its first seven elements. It has to be E because in a heap the smallest element, 1, must be a leaf, and all the leaves have to be clustered in the second half of the array. The answer is E. If you find this solution too tricky, you can get the same answer by running the data through the actual Heapsort algorithm, but that may require more work. ⏎

4.5. Hashing

Hashing is a method for storing information in which the value of an element (or the value of the key of an element) translates directly into its location in a *hash table*. Ideally, hashing provides instantaneous access to data (more precisely, the search time is constant regardless of the number of elements).

A typical hash table is a one-dimensional array of fixed size. Some elements of the array contain stored information, others may be empty. A *hash function* is provided that translates the value of an element into an integer in the range from 0 to *size*-1, which serves as a subscript into the array.

Hash tables are similar to lookup tables, but not quite the same. In a lookup table, the function that converts values into subscripts is always a one-to-one function, so each element's value is mapped onto a unique subscript into the table and therefore can be found without any ambiguity.

In hash tables, different values can be mapped into the same location in the table (i.e., the same subscript). These situations are called *collisions*.

Hash tables are used when lookup tables are not practical because they would take too much space. A good hash function spreads the values uniformly in the table, so that the number of collisions is minimized. Still, some method to resolve collisions is needed. The two most common methods are *probing* and *chaining*.

In *probing*, if we are trying to insert a new element into the hash table and its place is already occupied, we insert it into the next vacant slot in the same array. When we search for an element and the key or value doesn't match right away, we check the next consecutive slots until the element is found. There are variations of probing where the next tested slot is not necessarily the adjacent one but its location or offset is calculated in a more tricky way.

In *chaining*, each element of the hash table is not just one value, but a *bucket*, something that has its own storage. For example, each element in a hash table may be a pointer to the head node of a linked list. Finding a value in such a table involves first computing the subscript for the hash table, then traversing the corresponding linked list until the element is found. Or each element in the table may be a pointer to the root node of a binary search tree. In a good hash table the buckets remain small, containing just a few elements.

The hash function may do quite strange things to the key: cut it into pieces, rearrange, add, multiply, and so on, as long as it maps each allowed value into the legal range, from 0 to *size*-1. Often (especially in AP questions) division modulo *size* as the last step makes sure that the resulting subscript falls within the required range. A hash function should also be fairly easy to compute.

51

Consider designing a hash table that will hold information about conference participants, arranged by last name. The table will have 26 slots and hold about 1000 names, with collisions resolved through chaining with linked-list buckets. Two hash functions are being considered:

Function 1:

```
int Hash(const apstring & name)
{
    return name[0] - 'A';
}
```

Function 2:

```
int Hash(const apstring & name)
{
    int i, sum = 0;
    for (i = 0; i < name.length(); i++)
        sum += name[i] - 'A';

    return sum % 26;
}
```

Which of the following statements best represents the reason for choosing one version of the hash function over the other?

(A) Function 1 should be chosen because it is easier to compute.

(B) Function 1 should be chosen because it is easier to find the target name in the corresponding bucket.

(C) Function 2 should be chosen because it distributes the names more evenly between the buckets.

(D) Function 2 should be chosen because it places any two names that differ by one letter into different buckets.

(E) Neither function is appropriate because the range of returned values should be from 0 to 999.

☞ B, D, and E are just fillers: the hash function has nothing to do with searching within buckets, names differing by one letter are not a particularly common or important special case, and the range should be from 0 to 25, not from 0 to 999. A and C are potentially useful considerations, but since the table has pretty large buckets (about 40 elements, on average) the uniformity consideration is far more important here than the ease of computing. Function 1 places all names that start with the same letter in the same bucket, so the 'S' bucket may have 100 names while the 'X' bucket may have none. It will take much more time to traverse the long lists that correspond to the most frequent letters of the alphabet than to compute a longer version of the hash function. Besides, Function 2 is not all that difficult to compute. **The answer is C.** ⏎

4.6. Big-O Analysis

In previous chapters we have several times said things like "the number of required comparisons is approximately proportional to n^2" or "the running time is roughly proportional to log n." What exactly does "approximately" or "roughly" mean? "Big-O" provides a formal definition and notation for the concept of *order of growth*.

If we have two functions, $f(n)$ and $g(n)$, and the ratio $f(n)/g(n)$ approaches a positive constant as n increases without bound, then we can say that f and g have the same order of growth, and we can write:

$$f(n) = O(g(n))$$

The order of growth definition disregards a constant factor: $f(n) = O(k \cdot f(n))$ for any constant $k > 0$.

If $f(n)$ is a polynomial of degree k, then $f(n) = O(n^k)$.

For example,

$$\frac{n(n-1)}{2} = \frac{n^2}{2} - \frac{n}{2} = O(n^2)$$

Indeed,

$$\frac{\frac{n^2}{2} - \frac{n}{2}}{n^2} = \frac{1}{2} - \frac{1}{2n} \;\rightarrow\; \frac{1}{2}, \text{ as } n \text{ increases.}$$

In the analysis of algorithms, an integer n defines the size of a task: the number of elements in an array to be sorted; the number of nodes in a linked list, binary search tree or heap; or the number of elements stored in a hash table, queue, or stack, and so on. The time or space requirements for an algorithm can be expressed in terms of big-O of n. We use several standard reference functions to which we compare the rates of growth. The most common reference functions, listed here in increasing order, are:

1 (constant)
log *n*
n (linear)
n log n
n^2 (quadratic)
...

Most often we are interested in the running time. Table 4-1 shows big-O time requirements for some of the common algorithms discussed earlier. The table assumes that the algorithm is implemented in an optimal way and lists the <u>average</u> big-O performance. There may be best-case and worst-case scenarios where big-O is different. These differences are addressed in Table 4-2.

There are also rules of thumb, but <u>you have to use them with caution.</u>

If an algorithm takes a single loop, it's either <u>linear</u> for straightforward sequential processing or <u>logarithmic</u> for divide-and-conquer methods. If an algorithm takes nested loops, it's either <u>quadratic</u> for straightforward sequential iterations over a square or a triangle or "<u>*n* log *n*</u>" for an algorithm with a divide-and-conquer component.

The only "*n* log *n*" algorithms studied in the AP program are Mergesort, Quicksort, and Heapsort.

Table 4-2 shows the average, best, and worst cases for common algorithms. The worst case, in general, assumes that the algorithm is running on the data that takes the longest time to process.

Table 4-1. Big-O Examples for Common Algorithms

Big-O	Algorithm
$O(1)$ — "constant"	Appending an element at the end of an array Appending a node at the head of a linked list Push and pop operations for a stack Enqueue and dequeue operations for a queue Retrieval/insertion in a lookup table Retrieval/insertion in a hash table
$O(\log n)$ — "logarithmic"	Binary Search in a sorted array Search and insertion in a binary search tree Retrieval/insertion in a heap
$O(n)$ — "linear"	Sequential search in an array Traversals of lists or trees with n nodes Calculating sums or products of n elements, e.g. $n!$
$O(n \log n)$ — "n-log-n"	Mergesort Quicksort Heapsort
$O(n^2)$ — "quadratic"	Selection Sort and Insertion Sort Traversals of n by n matrices Algorithms that take nested loops: $1 \le k < n, 0 \le i < k$ (e.g., finding duplicate values in an array)

Table 4-2. Best, Average, and Worst Case Big-O's

	Best case	Average case	Worst case
Sequential Search	$O(1)$ — found right away	$O(n)$ — found on average in the middle	$O(n)$
Binary Search	$O(1)$ — found right away	$O(\log n)$	$O(\log n)$
Hash table search	$O(1)$ — found right away	$O(1)$ — small fixed-length buckets	$O(n)$ — table degenerated into one or two buckets
Search in a binary search tree	$O(1)$ — found right away	$O(\log n)$	$O(n)$ — tree degenerated into nearly a list
Selection Sort	$O(n^2)$	$O(n^2)$	$O(n^2)$
Insertion Sort	$O(n)$ — array already sorted	$O(n^2)$	$O(n^2)$
Mergesort	$O(n \log n)$	$O(n \log n)$	$O(n \log n)$
Quicksort	$O(n \log n)$	$O(n \log n)$	$O(n^2)$ — pivot is consistently chosen far from the median value, e.g., the array is already sorted and the first element is chosen as pivot
Heapsort	$O(n \log n)$	$O(n \log n)$	$O(n \log n)$
Insert a value into a heap	$O(1)$ — the value is the smallest in the heap	$O(\log n)$	$O(\log n)$

52

The following function eliminates consecutive nodes with duplicate values from a linked list. For example, A→B→B→B→C→A→A becomes A→B→C→A.

```
void SkipDuplicates(Node * head)
{
    Node * p = head;
    Node * p2;
    Node * temp;

    while (p != NULL)
    {
        p2 = p->next;
        while (p2 != NULL && p2->info == p->info)
        {
            temp = p2->next;
            delete p2;
            p2 = temp;
        }
        p->next = p2;
        p = p->next;
    }
}
```

Which of the following best describes the best-case and the worst-case running time for SkipDuplicates on a list with n nodes?

	Best case:	*Worst case*:
(A)	$O(1)$	$O(n)$
(B)	$O(n)$	$O(n)$
(C)	$O(1)$	$O(n^2)$
(D)	$O(n)$	$O(n^2)$
(E)	$O(n^2)$	$O(n^2)$

No matter what exactly the "best case" is, the function has to examine every node of the list. The running time cannot possibly be constant; therefore, A and C are wrong answers. There is a case when all the nodes are different. In that case the inner loop is simply skipped, and we end up with a simple traversal of the list in one sequential loop. The running time in that case is $O(n)$, so E is not the right answer, either. We are left with B and D. This example is an exception to the rule of thumb: it has nested loops, so you might think the worst time might be $O(n^2)$. But this function eliminates <u>consecutive</u> duplicate values, not all duplicate values. The trick is that the outer loop doesn't necessarily go to the next node, but can jump over all the removed nodes. Even when all the nodes of the list are the same, each node is visited only once. We did warn you to use the rules of thumb with caution, didn't we? The answer is B.

Chapter 5. Free-Response Questions: Annotated Solutions

The material for this chapter is on our web site:

`http://www.skylit.com/beprepared/fr.html`

These pages include links to free-response questions from recent years, one or several annotated solutions for each question, and comments on grading.

Chapter 6. Case Study

The material for this chapter is on our web site:

`http://www.skylit.com/beprepared/casestudy.html`

These pages include a brief review, links to the *Case Study* materials, and practice questions.

Practice Exams

COMPUTER SCIENCE A
SECTION I

Time — 1 hour and 15 minutes
Number of questions — 40
Percent of total grade — 50

1. Assuming that c and d are Boolean variables, the expression

    ```
    !c || d
    ```

    is equivalent to which of the following?

    (A)   !(c && d)
    (B)   c && !d
    (C)   !(c || !d)
    (D)   !(c && !d)
    (E)   !(!c && d)

2. What values of ch make the Boolean expression

    ```
    (ch != 'a' || ch != 'b' || ch != 'c')
    ```

    false?

      I. ch = 'a'
     II. ch = 'b'
    III. ch = 'x'

    (A)   I only
    (B)   II only
    (C)   III only
    (D)   I, II, and III
    (E)   None of the above

3. Given the declarations

    ```
    const int p = 5;
    int q = 3;
    ```

    which of the following expressions evaluate to 7.5?

    ```
    I.   double(p) * double(q) / 2;
    II.  double(p) * double(q / 2);
    III. double(p * q / 2);
    ```

    (A) I only
    (B) II only
    (C) I and II
    (D) I, II, and III
    (E) None of the above

4. What value is returned by the call Compute(10,3,7) for the function Compute below?

    ```
    int Compute(int a, int b, int c)
    {
        if (a == c + b)
            return (a - b);
        else if (a - c == 3)
        {
            if ( b > c)
                return b;
            else
                return -c;
        }
        return 0;
    }
    ```

    (A) 0
    (B) 3
    (C) 7
    (D) -3
    (E) -7

Questions 5-6 refer to the following code segment:

```
do
{
    switch (k % 10)
    {
        case 0:   cout << (90 + k) << ' ';  break;
        case 1:   cout << 91 << ' ';        break;
        case 2:   cout << 92 << ' ';        break;
        case 3:   cout << 93 << ' ';        break;
        case 4:   cout << 94 << ' ';        break;
        case 5:   cout << 95 << ' ';        break;
        default:  cout << (90 + k) << ' ';  break;
    }
    k++;
} while (k % 2 != 0);
```

Consider the following possible values of k:

    I.   k = 10
   II. k = 21
  III. k = 36

5.   Which of the above values of k results in an output that contains 91?

    (A)   I only
    (B)   II only
    (C)   III only
    (D)   I and II
    (E)   I and III

6.   Which of the above values of k results in two consecutive integers displayed?

    (A)   I only
    (B)   II only
    (C)   III only
    (D)   I and II
    (E)   I and III

7.   Which of the following correctly describes one of the differences in usage between variables and symbolic constants in a C++ program?

    (A)   A variable can be passed as an argument to a function while a constant cannot.
    (B)   A variable can be local but a constant is always global.
    (C)   A constant cannot be of double data type; a variable can.
    (D)   A constant cannot appear on the left-hand side of the += operator.
    (E)   A constant's name must use all capital letters.

8. Consider the function

```
void FunX(int & x, int y)
{
    int f = 2;

    x += f * y;
    y++;
    y = x - y;
}
```

Assuming

```
int g = -10, h = 8;
```

what are the values of g and h after FunX(g,h) is called?

```
        g      h
        ----------
(A)    -10     8
(B)     6      8
(C)     6     -3
(D)     6    -10
(E)    -10   -18
```

Questions 9-10 refer to the function Smile below:

```
void Smile(int n)
{
    int k;

    if (n == 0)
        return;
    for (k = 1; k <= n; k++)
        cout <<"smile!";
    Smile(n-1);
}
```

9. What is the output when `Smile(4)` is called?

    (A) `smile!`
    (B) `smile!smile!`
    (C) `smile!smile!smile!`
    (D) `smile!smile!smile!smile!`
    (E) `smile!smile!smile!smile!smile!smile!smile!smile!smile!smile!`

10. When `Smile(4)` is called, how many times will `Smile` actually be called, including the initial call?

    (A) 2
    (B) 3
    (C) 4
    (D) 5
    (E) 10

11. Consider the following declarations:

```
struct APTestResult
{
    apstring subject;
    int score;
};

struct APScholar
{
    apstring name;
    int id;
    apvector<APTestResult> exams;
};

apvector<APScholar> list(100);
```

Which of the following correctly refers to the third AP score of the sixth AP Scholar in `list`?

    (A) `list[5].exams[2].score;`
    (B) `list.exams.score[5,2];`
    (C) `list.exams.score[5][2];`
    (D) `list.exams[5].score[2];`
    (E) `list[5]exams[2]score;`

12. Consider the following function:

```
int ModX(int x, int y)
{
    h = x - y;
    return x % y;
}
```

If it is included as part of a larger program that compiles and executes correctly, which of the following statements will be true?

    I.   ModX has a side effect since h is not locally declared.

   II.   h must be an integer since x and y are integers.

  III.   h must be a global constant.

  (A)   I only
  (B)   II only
  (C)   III only
  (D)   I and II
  (E)   None

13. What is the value of v[4] after the following code is executed?

```
int i;
int d = 1;
apvector<int> v(8,1);

for (i = 0; i < v.length(); i++)
{
    d *= 2;
    v[i] += d;
}
```

  (A)   16
  (B)   32
  (C)   33
  (D)   64
  (E)   65

14. Consider the following three code segments:

    I.
    ```
    int  i = 1;
    while (i <= 10)
    {
        cout << i;
        i += 2;
    }
    ```

    II.
    ```
    int i = 1;
    do
    {
        cout << i;
        i += 2;
    } while (i < 11);
    ```

    III.
    ```
    int i;
    for (i = 0; i < 10; i++)
    {
        i++;
        cout << i;
    }
    ```

    Which of the three segments produce the same output?

    (A)   I and II only
    (B)   II and III only
    (C)   I and III only
    (D)   I, II, and III
    (E)   All three outputs are different

15. Which of the following best describes the appropriate postcondition for the function `PropertyX` below?

    ```
    bool PropertyX(const apvector<int> & v)
    // precondition: v.length() >= 2
    // postcondition: < ... >
    {
        bool flag = false;
        int i;

        for (i = 0; i < v.length() - 1; i++)
            flag = flag || (v[i] == v[i+1]);
        return flag;
    }
    ```

    (A)   Returns `true` if the elements of v are sorted in ascending order, `false` otherwise.
    (B)   Returns `true` if the elements of v are sorted in descending order, `false` otherwise.
    (C)   Returns `true` if v has two elements with the same value, `false` otherwise.
    (D)   Returns `true` if all elements in v have different values, `false` otherwise.
    (E)   Returns `true` if v has two adjacent elements with the same value, `false` otherwise.

16. Assuming that a and b are Boolean variables, when is the following expression true?

```
!(!a || b) || (!a && b)
```

(A) If and only if a is equal to b
(B) If and only if a is not equal to b
(C) If and only if both a and b are true
(D) If and only if both a and b are false
(E) Never

17. Consider the following function:

```
apstring SpaceBetween(const apstring & s, const apstring & t)
// precondition:  <...>
// postcondition: Returns a string in which the apstrings
//                s and t are concatenated together with
//                one space added between them.
{
    char space = ' ';        // A single space
    s += space;
    return s + t;
}
```

Which of the following best describes the behavior of SpaceBetween?

(A) The function compiles without errors and works as specified.
(B) The function works as specified only if s and t are non-empty strings.
(C) The function always returns a string that consists of one space.
(D) The function returns s and t concatenated, but does not insert a space between them.
(E) The compiler reports an error for this function.

18. Consider the following code segment:

```
if (denom != 0 && val / denom > limit)
    Process(denom, val);
else
    Discard(denom, val);
```

Which of the following code segments is equivalent to the one above?

I.
```
if (val / denom > limit && denom != 0)
    Process(denom, val);
else
    Discard(denom, val);
```

II.
```
if (denom == 0 || val / denom <= limit)
    Discard(denom, val);
else
    Process(denom, val);
```

III.
```
if (denom == 0)
{
    if (val / denom <= limit)
        Discard(denom, val);
}
else
    Process(denom, val);
```

(A)   I only
(B)   II only
(C)   III only
(D)   I and II
(E)   II and III

19. Consider the following function:

```
apstring MatchLetters(const apstring & str1,
                                 const apstring & str2)
{
    int i;
    apstring ans = "";

    int len = str1.length();
    if (len > str2.length())
        len = str2.length();

    for (i = 0; i < len; i++)
    {
        if (str1[i] != str2[i])
            ans += str1[i];
    }
    return ans;
}
```

What result is returned when `MatchLetters("Alaska", "Alabama")` is called?

(A)   3
(B)   "sk"
(C)   "ska"
(D)   "Ala"
(E)   Run-time subscript-out-of-bounds error

20. Consider the following function with two missing statements:

```
int AddOdds(const apvector<int> & A, int n)
// precondition:  1 <= n <= A.length()
// postcondition: Returns the sum of all positive odd values
//                among the first n elements of A.
{
    int i, sum = 0;
    < statement 1 >
    {
        < statement 2 >
            sum += A[i];
    }
    return sum;
}
```

Which of the following are appropriate replacements for < *statement 1* > and < *statement 2* > so that the function works as specified?

	< *statement 1* >	< *statement 2* >
(A)	`for (i = 1; i < n; i += 2)`	`if (A[i] > 0)`
(B)	`for (i = 0; i < n; i++)`	`if (A[i] > 0 && A[i] % 2 != 0)`
(C)	`for (i = 1; i <= n; i += 2)`	`if (A[i] > 0)`
(D)	`for (i = 0; i <= n; i++)`	`if (A[i] % 2 != 0)`
(E)	None of the above	

Questions 21-22 refer to the following function:

```
int Mystery(int a, int & b)
{
    cout << a << ' ';
    if (a <= b)
    {
        b--;
        Mystery(a+5, b);
    }
    return (a + b);
}
```

21. Assuming that integer variables x = 0 and y = 16 are declared, what is the output when Mystery(x, y) is called?

    (A)   0 5
    (B)   0 5 10
    (C)   0 5 10 15
    (D)   0 5 10 15 20
    (E)   12

22. Assuming that integer variables p = 1 and q = 3 are declared, what is the value of q after the statement

    ```
    q = Mystery(p, q);
    ```

    is executed?

    (A)   3
    (B)   5
    (C)   7
    (D)   8
    (E)   11

23. Consider the three code segments below:

```
I.    apvector<char> A(10), B(10);
      int k;
      for (k = 0; k < 10; k++)
      {
          A[k] = '*';
          B[k] = '*';
      }

II.   apvector<char> A(10, '*');
      apvector<char> B(A);

III.  apvector<char> A(10), B;
      int k;
      for (k = 0; k < 10; k++)
          A[k] = '*';
      B = A;
```

Which of these code segments correctly sets all ten elements in both arrays to `'*'`?

(A)   I only
(B)   I and II only
(C)   I and III only
(D)   III only
(E)   I, II, and III

Questions 24-25 refer to the following function:

```
void SortX(apvector<int> & A, int n)
{
    int i, k;
    int saved;

    for (i = 1; i < n; i++)
    {
        saved = A[i];
        for (k = i - 1; k >= 0; k--)
        {
            if (A[k] <= saved) break;
            A[k+1] = A[k];
        }
        A[k+1] = saved;
    }
}
```

24. SortX can be best described as:

(A)   Selection Sort
(B)   Insertion Sort
(C)   Quicksort
(D)   Mergesort
(E)   Incorrect implementation of a sorting algorithm

25. Assuming that the first six elements in A are 6 3 8 2 9 4, what are the values in A after two passes through the outer for loop in SortX(A,6)?

    (A)   2 3 4 6 8 9
    (B)   2 3 4 6 9 8
    (C)   3 6 8 2 9 4
    (D)   9 8 6 2 3 4
    (E)   8 6 3 2 9 4

26. Consider the following function:

```
int LinearSearch(const apvector <int> & A, int target)
// precondition:  A is filled with values.
// postcondition: Returns the index of the first element that
//                has the same value as target, or -1 if such
//                element is not found.
{
    int i;

    for (i = A.length(); i > 0; i--)
    {
        if (A[i] == target)
            return i;
    }
    return -1;
}
```

When will LinearSearch NOT work as specified?

    (A)   Every time the function is called
    (B)   When the target value is the first element in the array
    (C)   When the target value is the last element in the array
    (D)   When the target value is not in the array
    (E)   When the target value appears multiple times in the array

27. Which of the following is NOT a good reason to use comments in programs?

    (A)   To document the names of the programmer and the date of the last change
    (B)   To document a function's requirements for correct operation
    (C)   To explain a convoluted piece of code
    (D)   To document which members of a class are private
    (E)   To describe what an overloaded class member operator does

28. *Top-down* programming methodology is best characterized by:

    (A)   Writing header files before implementation files
    (B)   First coding functions that implement higher-level tasks, using temporary "stubs" for lower-level functions
    (C)   Having the project set up by a system analyst, then dividing the work among programmers
    (D)   Assembling the modules of the program from reusable components
    (E)   Designing data structures first and functions later

Questions 29-30 refer to the following function:

```
int CountX(const apmatrix<int> & m)
{
    int r, c;
    int sum = 0;

    for (r = 0; r < m.numrows(); r++)
        for (c = 0; c < m.numcols(); c++)
            sum += m[r][c] + r + c;

    return sum;
}
```

29. Given the declaration

    ```
    apmatrix<int> m(3,5,1);
    ```

    what value is returned by the call CountX(m)?

    (A)   10
    (B)   15
    (C)   30
    (D)   45
    (E)   60

30. If square is declared as apmatrix<int> square(n,n,0), where n is a positive integer, how many times is the statement sum += ... in CountX executed when CountX(square) is called?

    (A) n
    (B) $n(n-1)$
    (C) $(n-1)(n-1)$
    (D) $n(n+1)/2$
    (E) n^2

Questions 31-32 are concerned with a database for a travel agency. The agency wants to keep track of all its customers over the past five years, their dates of travel, and the destinations of their trips. Suppose the average number of trips per customer over the five-year time period is 5. Two designs are being considered for this application:

Design 1:
An array of customers, sorted by customer's name, and a matrix of trips. Each element of the array holds the customer's name, the number of trips made by that customer, and an index to a row of the matrix. Each row of the matrix holds the descriptions of all trips for one customer, sorted by date.

Design 2:
An array of trips sorted by date. Each element of the array holds the customer's name and the description of the trip.

31. Which of the following operations can be implemented more efficiently using Design 1 rather than Design 2?

    I.   Finding and reporting all the trips for a customer with a given name
    II.   Listing all customers who made eight or more trips in a given calendar year
    III.   Reporting how many trips fell on a given date

    (A)   I only
    (B)   II only
    (C)   I and II
    (D)   II and III
    (E)   I, II, and III

32. Suppose that in this database the number of bytes reserved for a customer name is the same for all customers and that it is the same as the number of bytes reserved for the description of each trip in both Design 1 and Design 2. Recall that the database holds, on average, 5 trips per customer. Suppose the number of columns in the matrix in Design 1 (that is, the number of trips that it can hold per customer) is n. Which of the following is the largest value of n for which Design 1 still saves space over Design 2?

    (A)   5
    (B)   6
    (C)   8
    (D)   10
    (E)   15

Questions 33-35 involve reasoning about structures and classes used in an implementation of a library catalog system. A structure `BookInfo` holds information about a particular book and a class `LibraryBook` helps to handle multiple copies of a book on library shelves:

```
struct BookInfo
{
    apstring title;
    apstring author;
    int numPages;
};

class LibraryBook
{
  public:
    // Constructors:
    < Not shown >

    bool CheckOut();
                // If there are copies on shelf, decrements
                //   the number of copies left and returns
                //   true; otherwise returns false

    void PrintTitle(ostream & os) const;
                // Prints the title of the book to os

    int GetNumCopies() const;
                // Returns the number of copies on shelf

    void SetNumCopies(int nCopies);
                // Sets the number of copies on shelf

    int GetNumPages() const;
                // Returns the number of pages in the book

    < Other functions not shown >

  private:
    BookInfo myInfo;
    int myNumCopies;    // Number of copies on shelf

    apstring GetTitle() const;
                // Returns the title of the book

    < Other members not shown >
};
```

33. If `catalog` is declared in a client program as

    ```
    apvector<LibraryBook> catalog;
    ```

    which of the following statements will correctly display the title of the third book in `catalog`?

    I.   `catalog[2].PrintTitle(cout);`
    II. `cout << catalog[2].GetTitle();`
    III. `cout << catalog[2].myInfo.title;`

    (A) I only
    (B) II only
    (C) III only
    (D) I and II
    (E) II and III

34. Which of the code segments will correctly complete the CheckOut() function below?

```
bool LibraryBook::CheckOut()
// postcondition: If there are copies on shelf, decrements the
//                number of copies left and returns true;
//                otherwise returns false.
{
    < Missing code >
}
```

I.
```
if (GetNumCopies() == 0)
    return false;
else
{
    SetNumCopies(GetNumCopies() - 1);
    return true;
}
```

II.
```
int n = GetNumCopies();
if (n == 0)
    return false;
else
{
    SetNumCopies(n-1);
    return true;
}
```

III.
```
if (myNumCopies == 0)
    return false;
else
{
    myNumCopies--;
    return true;
}
```

(A)   I only
(B)   II only
(C)   I and II
(D)   I and III
(E)   I, II, and III

35. Consider the function below with a missing statement:

```
int TotalPages(const apvector<LibraryBook> & catalog)
// postcondition: Returns the total number of pages in all books
//                 in catalog that are on the shelves.
{
    int k;
    int total = 0;

    for (k = 0; k < catalog.length(); k++)
    {
        < statement >
    }
    return total;
}
```

Which of the following replacements for < *statement* > completes the function as specified?

(A)   `total += catalog[k].myNumCopies * catalog[k].myInfo.numPages;`
(B)   `total += catalog[k].GetNumCopies() * catalog[k].numPages;`
(C)   `total += catalog[k].(myNumCopies * myInfo.numPages);`
(D)   `total += catalog[k].GetNumCopies() * catalog[k].GetNumPages();`
(E)   None of the above

36. Consider the following function:

```
int Search(const apvector<int> & A, int target)
// precondition:  A[0] ... A[A.length() - 1] are
//                 sorted in ascending order.
// postcondition: Returns the location of the target
//                 value in the array, or -1 if not found.
{
    int first = 0;
    int middle;
    int last = A.length() - 1;

    while (first <= last)
    {
        middle = (first + last) / 2;
        if (target == A[middle])
            return middle;
        if (target < A[middle])
            last = middle;
        else
            first = middle;
    }
    return -1;
}
```

This function fails to work as expected under certain conditions. If the array has five elements with values 3 4 35 42 51, which of the following values of `target` would make this function fail?

(A)   3
(B)   4
(C)   35
(D)   42
(E)   51

Questions 37-40 refer to the *Case Study*. These questions can be found at:

        http://www.skylit.com/beprepared/a1mc.html

COMPUTER SCIENCE A
SECTION II

Time — 1 hour and 45 minutes
Number of questions — 4
Percent of total grade — 50

1. Some airline companies have a "hub" — a city which is their base of operations. The hub is usually located somewhere in the middle of the airline's route system, so that the average distance from the hub to all other cities is fairly small and most cities are within reach of the hub.

    In this question all the cities served by an airline are represented in an array `apvector<City> cityList`, where `City` is the following structure:

    ```
    struct City
    {
        apstring name;
        Point location;
        double avgDist;
    };
    ```

    The data member `location` represents the location of the city. Assume that the function

    ```
    double Distance(const Point & loc1, const Point & loc2);
    ```

    is provided. It returns the distance between two different points or zero if the points happen to be the same.

    (a) Write a function `FillAvgDist` as started below. The function takes a list of cities and for each city calculates the average of the distances between that city and all other cities in the list. The result is stored in the `avgDist` data element of each city. You may assume that the data type `Point` is defined and that the function `Distance` works as specified.

    ```
    void FillAvgDist(apvector<City> & cityList)
    // precondition:  All elements in cityList represent cities.
    //                 cityList.length() >= 2
    // postcondition: The avgDist data element in each city
    //                 in cityList is set to the average of
    //                 the distances from that city to all
    //                 other cities in cityList.
    ```

(b) Write a function `HubCity` as started below. This function takes a list of cities, obtains the average distances from each city to other cities by calling `FillAvgDist`, and then finds and returns the city with the smallest average distance from the others. Assume that `FillAvgDist` works as specified regardless of what you wrote in Part (a).

```
City HubCity (apvector<City> & cityList)
// precondition:   All elements in cityList represent cities.
//                 cityList.length() >= 2
// postcondition: The city with the smallest average distance
//                 to other cities is found and returned.
```

(c) Let us call the average distance from the hub to the other cities the "radius." Write a function `LongFlight` that takes a list of cities and builds another list, made of those cities that are farther away from the hub than twice the radius. The function returns the number of cities in the newly created list. Assume that the function `HubCity` works as specified, regardless of what you wrote in Part (b), and that the city returned by `HubCity` already has the data element `avgDist` set to the radius. Also assume that the function `Distance` is provided, as described above.

```
int LongFlight (apvector<City> & cityList,
                        apvector<City> & farCityList)
// precondition:  All elements in cityList represent cities
//                served by an airline.
//                cityList.length() >= 2
//                farCityList.length() >= cityList.length()
// postcondition: The hub city is found and all the cities
//                from cityList whose distance from the hub is
//                greater than (2 * average distance) are copied
//                into farCityList.
//                Returns the number of cities placed into
//                farCityList.
```

2. The text of a story (a collection of words) is stored in a text file. The first line of the file contains the number of words in the story; the lines that follow contain the words. Assume that the file does not contain punctuation marks, that a line may hold several words, and that words cannot be split between lines. For example:

```
8
I do not like
green eggs
and ham
```

Consider a class `Story` that represents a collection of words and implements a few functions that handle such text. The class represents a story as an `apvector` of `apstring` elements. The class has a constructor that reads a story from an open text file. Consider the following partial definition of the `Story` class:

```
class Story
{
  public:

    Story(istream & inFile);   // Constructor:
                               //    loads a story from inFile

    void WriteWord(ostream & outFile);
                               // Writes the next word from
                               //    myStoryWords[myCurrWord] to
                               //    the outFile

    void ReplaceTwoWords(const apstring & word1,
          const apstring & word2, const apstring & word3);
                               // Replaces all occurrences of
                               //    word1 followed by word2
                               //    with word3

    < Other member functions not shown >

  private:

    int myWordCount;       // Number of words in the story

    apvector<apstring> myStoryWords;
                           // Holds the words of the story

    int myCurrWord;        // Index of the current word
    int myCharCount;       // Number of chars already displayed
                           //   on the current line
    int myLineLength;      // The maximum number of characters
                           //   to be displayed per line
};
```

(a)   Complete the code for the constructor as started below.

```
Story::Story (istream & inFile)
  : myCurrWord(0), myCharCount(0), myLineLength(80)
// precondition:   inFile is open for reading.
// postcondition:  myCurrWord and myCharCount are initialized
//                 to 0, myLineLength is initialized to 80.
//                 myWordCount (the number of words in the story)
//                 is read from the first line of inFile.
//                 apvector myStoryWords is resized accordingly
//                 and the story words are read from inFile into
//                 myStoryWords.
```

(b)   Write the code for the member function WriteWord as started below. The function writes the current word from the story (the word indexed by myCurrWord) into the specified output stream. One space character is always written after the word. Before writing the word, check that there is enough room on the current line for the word and its trailing space. If there is not enough room on the current line, output endl and start the next line, placing the word and its trailing space there. Update myCharCount accordingly. Increment myCurrWord by 1.

```
void Story::WriteWord(ostream & outFile)
// precondition:   0 <= myCurrWord < myWordCount;
//                 outFile is open for writing.
// postcondition:  myStoryWords[myCurrWord], followed by
//                 one space character, is written to outFile.
//                 If the word and its trailing space do not fit
//                 on the current line, it is placed on a new
//                 line.  myCharCount is updated appropriately.
//                 myCurrWord is incremented by 1.
```

(c) Write the code for the member function `ReplaceTwoWords`, as started below. Given three words, `word1`, `word2`, and `word3`, the function searches for all occurrences of `word1` immediately followed by `word2` and replaces them with `word3`. For example, if `myWordCount` is 16 and `myStoryWords` contains

0	1	2	3	4	5	6	7
I	do	not	like	green	eggs	and	ham

8	9	10	11	12	13	14	15
I	do	not	like	them	Sam	I	am

the call `ReplaceTwoWords("not", "like", "love")` on that story should reduce `myWordCount` to 14 and set `myStoryWords` to

0	1	2	3	4	5	6	7
I	do	love	green	eggs	and	ham	I

8	9	10	11	12	13
do	love	them	Sam	I	am

Assume that `word1`, `word2`, and `word3` are always all different.

```
void Story::ReplaceTwoWords(const apstring & word1,
           const apstring & word2, const apstring & word3)
// precondition:  myWordCount >= 2
//                word1, word2, and word3 are three different
//                words.
// postcondition: All occurrences of word1 immediately followed
//                by word2 are found, and both words are removed
//                and replaced with word3.  myWordCount is
//                decreased accordingly.
```

3. A class `WordSearch` implements a puzzle of searching for words in a table filled with letters. Consider the following partial definition of the `WordSearch` class. The letters are stored in the `apmatrix myLetters`. A constructor is provided that initializes the dimensions of the matrix `myRows` and `myCols`, resizes the matrix accordingly, and fills it with random letters.

```
class WordSearch
{
  public:
    WordSearch (int rows, int cols);  // Constructor
    bool SearchDown(const apstring & word,
                                    int row, int col) const;
    bool SearchAll(const apstring & word,
                                    int row, int col) const;
    < Other member functions not shown >

  private:
    int myRows;             // Number of rows in myLetters
    int myCols;             // Number of cols in myLetters
    apmatrix<char> myLetters; // Holds letters for the puzzle
};
```

(a) Write the constructor that initializes `WordSearch`, as started below. The constructor sets all elements of the matrix `myLetters` to random letters. Assume that a function

```
    char RandomLetter();
```

is provided that returns a random character in the range from 'a' to 'z'.

```
WordSearch::WordSearch (int rows, int cols)
   : myRows(rows), myCols(cols), myLetters(rows, cols)
// postcondition: myRows and myCols are set to rows and cols
//                respectively, myLetters is resized to
//                rows, cols and filled with random letters.
```

(b) Write the code for the function `SearchDown` as started below. This function attempts to match a given word to the letters in `myLetters`, starting at a given position (*row, col*) and moving down. Assume that all the letters in `word` are lower case. The search is allowed to wrap around and return to the top row of the same column if it gets out of bounds at the bottom. The function returns true if all the letters in `word` matched successfully to letters in `myLetters` and false otherwise. For example, given the following contents of `myLetters`, the function `SearchDown` would return the following values:

```
    | 0 1 2 3 4 5                                     Returns:
 0  | e r e a o d      SearchDown("toy", 2, 4)          true
 1  | h a s u d e      SearchDown("seek", 4, 0)         false
 2  | i i t k t o      SearchDown("state", 1, 2)        true
 3  | e e a z o h      SearchDown("estate", 0, 2)       true
 4  | s k t n y c
```

```
bool WordSearch::SearchDown (const apstring & word,
                                    int row, int col) const
// precondition:  0 <= row < myRows and 0 <= col < myCols
//                word has at least one letter and
//                'a' <= word[k] <= 'z' for all letters in word.
// postcondition: Returns true if all letters in word match
//                letters in myLetters, starting at the row, col
//                position and going down with wrap-around to
//                the top row after the bottom row.
```

(c) Write the code for the function `SearchAll`, as started below. This function attempts to match a given word to the letters in `myLetters`, starting at a given position. You are allowed to move by one square up, down, left, or right to look for the next letter. Wrapping around borders is not allowed, but self-intersecting words are allowed, so you can reuse the letters already matched to another letter in `word`. The function returns true if a match for all letters is found and false otherwise. For example, given the following contents of `myLetters`, the function `SearchAll` would return the following values:

```
      | 0 1 2 3 4 5                                           Returns:
    0 | e r e r o m      SearchAll("toy", 2, 4)                 true
    1 | h a s d t e      SearchAll("seek", 4, 0)                true
    2 | i i t k t o      SearchAll("state", 1, 2)               false
    3 | e e a z o h      SearchAll("motordrome", 0, 5)  true
    4 | s k t n y c
```

One convenient algorithm for the `SearchAll` function uses recursion, as follows:

- If `word` has only one letter, the function returns `true` or `false` depending on the match in the starting position.
- Otherwise, if the first letter matches the one in the starting position, then:
  - Take the substring of `word`, starting from the second letter.
  - Try to match (recursively) that substring at any of the four adjacent positions that fall within the boundaries of the matrix.

```
bool WordSearch::SearchAll (const apstring & word,
                                      int row, int col) const
// precondition:  0 <= row < myRows and 0 <= col < myCols
//                word has at least one letter and
//                'a' <= word[k] <= 'z' for all letters in word.
// postcondition: Returns true if all letters in word match
//                a string of adjacent letters in myLetters.
//                An element in the matrix may have four
//                (inside), three (on a side), or two (in a
//                corner) adjacent elements.  Self-intersecting
//                strings are allowed.
```

4. This question refers to the *Case Study*. It can be found at

http://www.skylit.com/beprepared/a1fr.html

COMPUTER SCIENCE A
SECTION I

Time — 1 hour and 15 minutes
Number of questions — 40
Percent of total grade — 50

1. What is the output of the following program segment?

```
int num = 3;
while (num > 0)
    num--;
cout << num << endl;
```

    (A) 2 1 0
    (B) 2 1
    (C) 2
    (D) 0
    (E) -1

2. Which of the following is an example of an *Abstract Data Type*?

    (A) apmatrix<int>
    (B) enum Status {Ok, Warning, Error};
    (C) cout
    (D) An array of values, sorted in ascending order, and two functions: one that inserts a value and one that finds a given value
    (E) apvector<AnyType>

3. Assuming that x and y are int variables, the expression

    ```
    !(x <= y || y > 0)
    ```

    is equivalent to which of the following?

    (A) !(x <= y) || (y > 0)
    (B) x > y && y <= 0
    (C) x <= y || y > 0
    (D) x > y || y < 0
    (E) x <= y && y <= 0

4.   Which of the following statements about data types in C++ is FALSE?

(A)   A data type may determine how variables or constants of that type are stored in RAM while the program is running.

(B)   A data type may determine how calculations are performed on variables or constants of that type.

(C)   A data type may determine whether a variable of that type may be declared only as a global variable.

(D)   A data type may determine whether a variable of that type may be passed as an argument to a particular function.

(E)   A data type may determine the range of values for variables or constants of that type.

5.   Which of the following could serve as a postcondition in the following function?

```
int Process(double amt)
// precondition:  amt represents cost of goods
//                in dollars and cents.
// postcondition: <...>
{
    return int(amt * 100) % 100;
}
```

(A)   Returns the cent portion in amt.

(B)   Returns the number of whole dollars in amt.

(C)   Returns amt rounded to the nearest integer.

(D)   Returns amt truncated to the nearest integer.

(E)   Returns amt converted into cents.

6. Consider the following code segment where m is an integer variable:

```
while (m <= 0)
     m++;
if (m == 1)
     cout << "One";
else
     cout << "Many";
```

Which of the following code segments would produce the same output as the one above, regardless of the value of m?

I.
```
if (m <= 1)
     cout << "One";
else
     cout << "Many";
```

II.
```
if (m <= 0)
     m = 1;
switch (m)
{
   case 1:  cout << "One";  break;
   default: cout << "Many"; break;
}
```

III.
```
switch (m)
{
   case 1:  cout << "One";  break;
   default: cout << "Many"; break;
}
```

(A) I only
(B) II only
(C) I and II
(D) II and III
(E) I, II, and III

7. Suppose a function `FindPrimes` finds and places the first *n* primes into an array. Two versions of the function are being considered:

Version 1:
```
void FindPrimes(int n, apvector<int> & primes);
// precondition:  n > 0; A.length() >= n
// postcondition: A[0], ..., A[n-1] hold the first n primes.
// Example:       apvector<int> P(100);
//                FindPrimes(100, P);
```

Version 2:
```
apvector<int> FindPrimes(int n);
// precondition:  n > 0
// postcondition: Returns an apvector of size n
//                with its elements holding the first n primes.
// Example:       apvector<int> P;
//                P = FindPrimes(100);
```

Which of the following statements is true?

(A)   Version 2 is not feasible because a function cannot return an `apvector`.

(B)   In Version 1 P is passed to `FindPrimes` by reference, and in Version 2 it is passed to `FindPrimes` by value.

(C)   Version 1 is less efficient because an apvector P of a given size has to be constructed before it is passed to the function.

(D)   Version 1 is more efficient because the use of Version 2 involves an assignment operator for `apvectors` which copies one array into another.

(E)   Only one of the two versions can be defined in the same program.

8. Consider the following function:

```
void Show (int wheels)
{
    switch (wheels % 5)
    {
      case 1: cout << "Unicycle has "; break;
      case 2: cout << "Bicycle has "; break;
      case 3: cout << "Tricycle has "; break;
      case 4: cout << "Car has "; break;
      default:  break;
    }
    cout << wheels % 5 << " wheel(s)" << endl;
}
```

What is the output when `Show(13)` is called?

(A)   Unicycle has 1 wheel(s)
(B)   Bicycle has 2 wheel(s)
(C)   Tricycle has 3 wheel(s)
(D)   Car has 4 wheel(s)
(E)   0 wheel(s)

Questions 9-10 use the following definitions:

```
apstring S = "Computer Science";

int Look (apstring & S, char ch)
{
    int pos, count = 0;

    while (S.find(ch) != npos)
    {
        pos = S.find(ch);
        S = S.substr(pos + 1, S.length() - pos - 1);
        count += (pos + 1);
    }
    return count;
}
```

9. What is the output of the statement cout << Look(S,'e') << endl; ?

   (A) 36
   (B) 16
   (C) 15
   (D) 7
   (E) 6

10. After the statement

   ```
   cout << Look(S,'e') << endl;
   ```

   is executed, what is the value of S?

   (A) Computer Science
   (B) r Science
   (C) nce
   (D) e
   (E) The empty string

11. What is the output from the following code segment?

```
int a = 3;
int b = 4;
int c = 0;

if (a == 10 && b/c == 1)
    c = 2 * b;
else
{
    c = 2 * a;
    cout << c << endl;
}
```

(A) Run-time division-by-zero error
(B) 0
(C) 6
(D) 8
(E) 20

12. Which of the following best defines *encapsulation*?

(A) Placing a class definition into a header file and all the code for its member functions into a separate implementation file
(B) Providing a default constructor, a copy constructor, and an overloaded assignment operator for a class
(C) Hiding the inner workings of a class from its clients by making all its data members private
(D) Placing all the code needed for a program into one file
(E) Creating a templated class that works with all built-in data types

13. Consider the following code segment:

```
int n;
cin >> n;

while (n >= 2)
    n = n/2 - 1;

while (n <= -2)
    n = n/2 + 1;

cout << n;
```

Which of the following is the list of all possible outputs?

(A) 0
(B) -1, 0
(C) 0, 1
(D) -1, 1
(E) -1, 0, 1

Questions 14-15 are concerned with the design options for a subscriber database for a magazine publisher. The publisher needs to keep track of the subscription expiration dates for subscribers to its three magazines. Two designs are being considered.

In Design 1, the database is represented as an array of subscribers. Each element in the array holds subscriber information (name, address, etc.) and a list of the three expiration dates for the three magazines, apvector<Date>. A special reserved value for the expiration date, such as 0/0, indicates that this subscriber doesn't subscribe to a particular magazine.

Design 2 uses two arrays: an array of subscribers, excluding subscription information, and a separate array of subscriptions. Each element in the subscriptions array is represented by the following structure:

```
struct MagSubscription
{
    int subscriberNum;  // Subscript into the subscriber array
    int mag;            // Magazine number 1, 2, or 3
    Date exp;           // Expiration date
};
```

14. Assuming that a MagSubscription structure takes 8 bytes and an apvector<Date> of length 3 takes 12 bytes, in which one of the following situations will Design 2 save memory over Design 1?

(A) Never
(B) The average number of subscriptions per customer is 2.5
(C) Magazine 1 is ten times more popular than Magazines 2 and 3 combined
(D) All subscriptions for a given subscriber renew in the same month and year
(E) Always

15. If the list of subscribers is arranged in no particular order, and the list of subscriptions in Design 2 is sorted in ascending order by expiration date, which of the following tasks can be implemented more efficiently using Design 1 rather than Design 2?

(A) Print mailing labels for renewal notices for all Magazine 1 subscribers whose subscriptions will expire next month
(B) Renew a subscription for a specified magazine for a given subscriber
(C) Count the number of current subscriptions to each of the three magazines
(D) Generate a list of all "loyal" customers who are subscribed to Magazine 1 for at least two years ahead
(E) Estimate the median remaining subscription time for all current subscriptions

16. Consider the two code segments below:

<table>
<tr><td align="center">Segment A</td><td align="center">Segment B</td></tr>
</table>

```
while (count < 10)          do
{                           {
    count++;                    count++;
}                           } while (count < 10);
cout << count << endl;      cout << count << endl;
```

For what initial value of count will the output of Segment A be different from the output of Segment B?

(A) When count is less than 0
(B) When count is 0
(C) When count is 1
(D) When count is 9
(E) When count is 10

17. Consider the following function:

```
void DoIt (apvector<char> & list)
{
    int j;
    int len = list.length() - 1;
    char temp;

    for (j = 0; j < len / 2; j++)
    {
        temp = list[j];
        list[j] = list[len - j];
        list[len - j] = temp;
    }
}
```

Which of the following best describes the task performed by this function?

(A) Reverse the order of elements in an array
(B) Sort an array
(C) Swap two arrays
(D) Swap the first and last elements of an array
(E) Swap the first and the last halves of an array

18. Consider the following two implementations of the function Sum:

I.
```
void Sum (int & x,  int & y)
{
    x += y;
    y += x;
}
```

II.
```
void Sum (int & x,  int & y)
{
    int s = x + y;
    x = s;
    y = s;
}
```

The two versions produce the same result if and ONLY if

(A) x is equal to 0
(B) y is equal to 0
(C) y is equal to x
(D) Sum is called as Sum(w, w), where w is a variable of the type int.
(E) Aliasing does not happen, that is Sum is called with x and y that do not refer to the same variable

19. What is the output from the following code?

```
int sum = 0, count, d = -1;
for (count = 10; count > 0; count--)
{
    sum += d;
    if (d > 0)
        d++;
    else
        d--;
    d = -d;
}
cout << sum;
```

(A)   0
(B)   5
(C)   -5
(D)   10
(E)   -10

Questions 20-21 refer to the following function:

```
void Fox(int x, int y)
{                                // Line  1
    if (x != y)                  // Line  2
    {                            // Line  3
        if (x < y)               // Line  4
        {                        // Line  5
            Fox(x, y - x);       // Line  6
        }                        // Line  7
        else                     // Line  8
        {                        // Line  9
            Fox(x - y, y);       // Line 10
        }                        // Line 11
    }                            // Line 12
    else                         // Line 13
        cout << y << ' ';        // Line 14
}                                // Line 15
```

20. What is the output of the call Fox(20,56)?

   (A)   4
   (B)   16
   (C)   20
   (D)   36
   (E)   Fox(20,36)

21. Which of the following changes will result in Fox(6,15) producing the output 15 9 3 ?

   (A)   Line 13 deleted, Line 14 moved after Line 1
   (B)   Line 13 deleted, Line 14 moved after Line 3
   (C)   Line 13 deleted
   (D)   Line 13 deleted, Line 14 moved after Line 6 and copied again after line 10
   (E)   Lines 13 and 14 moved after Line 2 in reverse order

22. Consider the following function:

```
void PrintX(const apstring & lead, int levels)
{
    if (levels <= 0)
        cout << endl;
    else
    {
        cout << lead;
        PrintX(lead + 'x', levels - 1);
    }
}
```

What is the output when `PrintX("ab", 2)` is called?

(A) abx

(B) ababx

(C) abxab

(D) ab
     xab

(E) abxab
     xab

23. A function that implements Binary Search in an array of integers is designed to work with an array sorted in ascending order. Under which of the following circumstances will the function find a given target value even when the array is not sorted?

   I.   The target value is located exactly in the middle of the array.

   II. The array is partially sorted: the smallest ten values are in ascending order at the beginning of the array and the target is among them.

   III. The array is partially sorted: all the values to the left of the target are smaller than the target and all the values to the right of the target are larger than the target.

(A) I only
(B) I and II
(C) I and III
(D) II and III
(E) I, II, and III

24. Consider the following function:

```
void ProcessMatrix(apmatrix<int> & M, int n)
// precondition: 1 <= n <= M.numrows(); n <= M.numcols()
{
    int r, c;
    int temp;

    for (r = 1; r < n; r++)
    {
        for (c = 0; c < r; c++)
        {
            temp = M[r][c];
            M[r][c] = M[c][r];
            M[c][r] = temp;
        }
    }
}
```

If S is a 3 by 3 matrix with values

```
8 1 6
3 5 7
4 9 2
```

what are the values in S after ProcessMatrix(S, 2) is called?

(A)   8 1 6
       3 5 7
       4 9 2

(B)   8 3 6
       1 5 7
       4 9 2

(C)   8 3 4
       1 5 9
       6 7 2

(D)   2 7 6
       9 5 1
       4 3 8

(E)   3 5 7
       8 1 6
       4 9 2

Questions 25-28 use structure `Track` and partially defined class `CD`:

```
struct Track
{
    apstring name;
    int duration;
};

class CD
{
  public:

    // Constructors:

    CD();
    CD(const apstring & title, int numTracks);
    CD(const apstring & title, const apstring & band,
            int numTracks, const apvector<Track> & songs);

    // Accessors and Modifiers:

    int TotalPlayTime() const;
    int GetDuration(int k) const;
        // precondition:  1 <= k <= myNumTracks
        // postcondition: Returns duration of the k-th track.

    void SetTrack (int k, const Track & t);

    < Other member functions not shown >

  private:
    apstring myTitle;
    apstring myBand;
    int myNumTracks;
    apvector<Track> myTracks;
};
```

25. Which one of the following declarations would be INVALID?

    (A) `Track tune;`
    (B) `apvector<Track> playList(20);`
    (C) `CD top("throwing copper", 13);`
    (D) `apvector<CD> favorites(7, "Live");`
    (E) `apmatrix<CD> rack(3, 40);`

26. Which of the following expressions would correctly refer to the duration of the *k*-th track inside the `TotalPlayTime` member function?

    (A) `GetDuration(k);`
    (B) `GetDuration(myTracks[k-1]);`
    (C) `myTracks.GetDuration(k);`
    (D) `myTracks[k-1].GetDuration();`
    (E) `myTracks[k-1].Track.duration;`

27. Which of the following best describes the purpose of the keyword `const` in front of `apvector<Track>` in the list of arguments for the constructor

```
CD::CD (const apstring & title, const apstring & band,
          int numTracks, const apvector<Track> & songs);
```

    (A)   Only a constant can be passed as this argument to this constructor.

    (B)   This constructor cannot change the size of `myTracks`.

    (C)   This constructor cannot change the size or the contents of `songs`.

    (D)   `songs` cannot be used in the initializer list for this constructor.

    (E)   Encapsulation

28. What is the result of the following code?

```
Track t;                                          // Line 1
t.name = "lightning crashes";                     // Line 2
t.duration = 200;                                 // Line 3
apvector<Track> tracks(13, t);                    // Line 4
CD live("throwing copper", "live", 13, tracks);   // Line 5
cout << live.TotalPlayTime();                      // Line 6
```

    (A)   Syntax error on Line 6

    (B)   Run-time subscript-out-of-bounds error

    (C)   0 is displayed

    (D)   200 is displayed

    (E)   2600 is displayed

29. Suppose a project comprises two files: an implementation file `myclass.cpp` that holds reusable code for `myclass`'s member functions, and a main program in a separate file `test.cpp`. Suppose we need to add a function `Process` that is not a member of class `myclass` but handles objects of type `myclass`. Which of the following best describes where the code for `Process` belongs?

    (A)   The code for `Process` should be added to `test.cpp` because `myclass.cpp` may contain only `myclass`'s member functions.

    (B)   The code for `Process` belongs in `test.cpp` because `myclass.cpp` is a reusable module.

    (C)   The code for `Process` belongs in `myclass.cpp` because `Process` handles objects of the type `myclass`.

    (D)   The code for `Process` belongs in `myclass.cpp` because it reduces compilation time when `test.cpp` is modified.

    (E)   It depends: if `Process` is general and can be used in many other projects, then it should be placed in `myclass.cpp`, but if it is specific to this particular project, then it belongs in `test.cpp`.

30. The function below supplies a check digit for a three-digit number to form a four-digit access code:

```
void AddCheckDigit(apvector<int> & pin)
// precondition:  pin[0], pin[1], and pin[2] hold digits
//                in the range from 0 to 9.
// postcondition: The check digit is computed
//                and placed into pin[3].
{
    pin[3] = (pin[0] + 2 * pin[1] + 3 * pin[2]) % 10;
}
```

Which of the following values in `pin` will get the same check digit as the one supplied for 5 2 3?

(A) 2 5 3
(B) 7 2 3
(C) 5 2 9
(D) 6 5 4
(E) 6 1 3

31. The function `MatchingBraces` below returns `true` if the string `expr` has no braces or has pairs of matching braces and `false` otherwise.

```
bool MatchingBraces(const apstring & expr)
{
    int k, count = 0;

    for (k = 0; k < expr.length(); k++)
        if (expr[k] == '{')
            count++;
        else if (expr[k] == '}')
        {
            < code >;
        }
    return count == 0;
}
```

Which of the following statements should be used in place of < *code* >?

(A) `count--;`
(B) `if (count > 0) count--; else return false;`
(C) `count = 0;`
(D) `if (count > 0) count = 0; else return false;`
(E) `if (count == 0) return true;`

For <u>Questions 32-34</u> consider the following partially defined class:

```
class Rectangle
{
  public:
    Rectangle (double w, double h);
      // Constructor: builds a rectangle of width w and
      //   height h with its center at the origin (0,0),
      //   its sides parallel to the sides of the screen

    void Move(double dx, double dy);
      // Moves this rectangle by dx horizontally and by dy
      //   vertically from its current position
      //   (moves to the right and down when dx and dy are
      //   positive and to the left and up when they are
      //   negative)

    void SetWidth(double w);
      // Sets new width keeping the center unchanged

    void SetHeight(double h);
      // Sets new height keeping the center unchanged

    void Rotate90();
      // Swaps width and height of this rectangle keeping
      //   the center unchanged

    double GetWidth();
      // Returns current width

    double GetHeight();
      // Returns current height

    void Draw();
      // Draws the border of this rectangle on the screen
      //   by setting the appropriate screen pixels to black

    < Other functions and data members not shown >
};
```

32. Which of the following member functions is NOT a modifier?

    (A) Move
    (B) SetWidth
    (C) SetHeight
    (D) Rotate90
    (E) Draw

33. Which of the following code fragments draws a 3 by 3 grid, such as the one below, on the screen?

I.
```
Rectangle R(1.0, 1.0);
int i, j;
for (i = 0; i < 3; i++)
{
    for (j = 0; j < 3; j++)
    {
        R.Move(double(i), double(j));
        R.Draw();
    }
}
```

II.
```
Rectangle R(3.0, 3.0);
R.Draw();
R.SetWidth(1.0);
R.Draw();
R.Rotate90();
R.Draw();
```

III.
```
Rectangle R(2.0, 2.0);
R.Draw();
R.Move(1.0, 0.0);
R.Draw();
R.Move(0.0, 1.0);
R.Draw();
R.Move(-1.0, 0.0);
R.Draw();
```

(A) I only
(B) II only
(C) III only
(D) I and II
(E) II and III

34. Consider the following function:

```
void Ornament(double d)
{
    if (d < 0.2)
        return;
    Rectangle s(d, d);
    s.Move(-d/2, -d/2);
    s.Draw();
    s.Move(d, d);
    s.Draw();
    Ornament(d/2);
}
```

Which of the following drawings is produced when Ornament(1) is called?

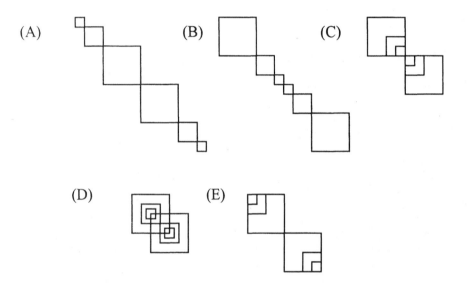

(A)   (B)   (C)

(D)   (E)

35. Which one of the following statements about constructors of the class SomeClass is true?

(A) If a local variable of the type SomeClass is declared in a function, the appropriate SomeClass constructor is called when that function is compiled.
(B) If a local variable is declared without any parameters, as in
        SomeClass someVar;
     then none of SomeClass's constructors is called.
(C) If a constructor takes arguments, it must have an initializer list.
(D) SomeClass cannot have two constructors with the same argument lists, that is, with the same number of arguments of the same types listed in the same order.
(E) If SomeClass has an apvector member, all of SomeClass's constructors must have initializer lists.

36. A program TEST has a function

```
bool LoadText(const apstring & fileName);
```

that opens and reads a text file. The program uses the following statement to open and read test.cpp:

```
bool status = LoadText("a:\test.cpp");
```

If this program fails to open test.cpp, which of the following is the most likely reason?

(A)   The function LoadText does not work as expected because a literal string is passed as an argument in place of an apstring.
(B)   The file test.cpp is used by another program.
(C)   A program cannot open its own source file.
(D)   The combination \t in the file name is interpreted as the tab character.
(E)   test.cpp is a binary file, not a text file.

Questions 37-40 refer to the *Case Study*. These questions can be found at:

http://www.skylit.com/beprepared/a2mc.html

COMPUTER SCIENCE A
SECTION II

Time — 1 hour and 45 minutes
Number of questions — 4
Percent of total grade — 50

1. The following structure represents information about an AP exam taken by a student:

```
struct APexam
{
    apstring subject;
    int level;    // 1 -- half year, 2 -- full year
    int grade;
};
```

A database of AP program participants represents each student in the following structure:

```
struct APstudent
{
    apstring name;
    apvector<APexam> exams;   // All exams taken by this student
};
```

(a) Write a function `AverageGrade` that calculates and returns the average grade on all AP exams for an AP student. Complete `AverageGrade` below the following header:

```
double AverageGrade(const APstudent & student)
// precondition:  exams data member in structure student
//                contains a list of all AP exams taken by
//                this student.  The list is not empty and
//                its length is the number of exams taken
//                by student.
// postcondition: Returns the average grade for all
//                AP exams taken by student.
```

(b) The College Board offers AP Scholar awards to students with grades of 3 or higher on
three or more AP Exams on full-year courses. Half-year courses are counted as half of
a full-year course. The College Board also grants AP Scholar with Honors awards to
students with grades of 3 or higher on four or more full-year exams (or the equivalent
mix of full- and half-year courses) and an average AP Exam grade of at least 3.25 on all
exams taken. Students may have low grades on some AP exams and still meet the
requirements for either award. This is summarized in the table below:

	AP Scholar	AP Scholar with Honors
Minimum grade that counts	3	3
Required number of courses not below min grade	3 years	4 years
Average grade on all AP exams taken	no effect	3.25
Number of exams below min grade	no effect	no effect

Write a function Award that returns the level of award earned by an AP student: 0 for
no award, 1 for the AP Scholar award and 2 for the AP Scholar with Honors award.
You may assume that AverageGrade works as specified regardless of what you wrote
in Part (a). Complete Award below the following header:

```
int Award(const APstudent & student)
// precondition:  exams data member in structure student
//                contains a list of all AP exams taken by
//                this student.  The list is not empty and
//                its length is the number of exams taken
//                by student.
// postcondition: The award level is computed and returned,
//                as follows: 0 for no award, 1 for AP Scholar,
//                and 2 for AP Scholar with Honors.
```

(c) Write a function `Stats` that takes a list of the AP program participants and calculates the percentages of students with no award, AP Scholars, and AP Scholars with Honors. In writing `Stats` you may assume that the function `Award` works as specified, regardless of what you wrote in Part (b). Complete `Stats` below the following header:

```
void Stats(const apvector<APstudent> & list, int numStudents,
                                  apvector<double> & percent)
// precondition:  list contains numStudents students,
//                their exam lists properly filled with data.
// postcondition: percent is resized to hold three elements.
//                percent[0], percent[1], and percent[2] are
//                filled with percentages of all students
//                from the list with no award, AP Scholars,
//                and AP Scholars with Honors, respectively.
```

2. Millions of web pages on the Internet are formatted in HTML, the HyperText Markup Language. HTML text contains embedded tags — formatting instructions delimited by the angular brackets < and >. The formatting tags usually come in pairs where the opening tag indicates the beginning of some formatting (e.g., italics, bold, underline) and the closing tag indicates the end of formatting. The closing tag contains the same keyword or instruction as the opening tag, but preceded by a slash (the ' / ' character). The following example shows a line of HTML text and illustrates the way it might be displayed on the screen:

```
The <I>quick</I> <B>brown</B> fox <B>jumps
<U>over</B> the lazy</U> dog
```

The *quick* **brown** fox **jumps <u>over** the lazy</u> dog

Processing HTML text may involve such tasks as removing HTML tags from the text or verifying that opening and closing tags come in matching pairs.

In this question we will deal only with one line of text represented as one `apstring`. We assume that this HTML line contains only complete tags: all '<' and '>' characters occur in pairs which properly delimit tags and do not otherwise occur inside tags or anywhere else in the text. The the segments of text formatted with different tags may overlap. For example, in the above example, the word "**over**", falls into the overlapping bold and underscored segments.

Recall that the `apstring` class has a member function `find` that finds a given character or a substring and returns its position or `npos` if not found. It also has the member function `substr`, which builds and returns a substring of a given length starting at a given position. Two `apstrings` can be concatenated using the + operator.

(a) Write a function `Remove` as started below. The function finds the first occurrence of a given substring in a text string and removes it. The function returns `true` if the substring was found and removed and `false` otherwise.

```
bool Remove(apstring & text, const apstring & str)
// precondition:  str is a non-empty string.
// postcondition: If str is found in text, its first occurrence
//                is removed from text and true is returned.
//                Otherwise, text remains unchanged and false
//                is returned.
```

(b) Write a function `RemoveFirstTag` as started below. The function finds the first tag in a given HTML text string and removes it. The function returns an `apstring` equal to the found tag (including the `<` and `>` brackets) or an empty string if no tags were found. You can assume that the function `Remove` works as specified regardless of what you wrote in Part (a).

```
apstring RemoveFirstTag(apstring & text)
// precondition:  text is a segment of HTML text which may
//                contain complete HTML tags.  A tag is any
//                substring starting with < and ending with
//                the closest >.
// postcondition: If an HTML tag is found in text, the first tag
//                is removed from text and the tag
//                (including the < and > brackets) is
//                returned.  Otherwise, text remains unchanged
//                and an empty string is returned.
```

(c) Write a function `RemoveAllTags`. The function assumes that a given text contains only complete simple tags, such as `<U>` and `</U>` or `<CITE>` and `</CITE>`, where a closing tag differs from the corresponding opening tag only by the `'/'` character after `'<'`. The function returns true if no tags were found in the text or if all tags come in matching pairs with a matching closing tag somewhere after an opening tag. You can assume that the functions `Remove` and `RemoveFirstTag` work as specified regardless of what you wrote in Parts (a) and (b).

`RemoveAllTags` removes all tags from the text if the pairs match and leaves the text unchanged if they don't. Therefore, your function has to work with a temporary copy of the text or save the original string. Recall that the `=` operator can be used to copy an `apstring`. `RemoveAllTags` can first find and remove the first tag (verifying that it is an opening tag), then build a matching closing tag and try to remove it. You can keep repeating this procedure for as long as any tags remain in the text.

Write `RemoveAllTags` below the following header:

```
bool RemoveAllTags(apstring & text)
// precondition:  text is a segment of HTML text which may
//                contain complete HTML tags.
// postcondition: If all HTML tags in text come in matching
//                opening-closing pairs, then all the tags are
//                removed from text and true is returned.
//                (If text has no tags, true is returned.)
//                If tags do not match (i.e., a closing tag
//                comes before the corresponding opening tag
//                or a closing tag is not found),
//                then text remains unchanged and false is
//                returned.
```

3. Optical Character Recognition (OCR) software interprets images of letters or digits scanned from documents. A simple OCR method, suitable for one font of fixed size, is called "template matching." A template is created for each character in the font. A template is a kind of numeric mask which has positive numbers (weights) in those places where the picture of the character is likely to have black pixels and negative weights where the picture is likely to have white space. For example, a template for 'A' may have the size 9 rows by 11 columns, and may use the weights shown on the picture below.

Template for 'A'

Digitized image of a character and a 9 by 11 template placed over it at position row = 2, col = 3

```
-1 -1 -1 -1 -1  0 -1 -1 -1 -1 -1

-1 -1 -1 -1  0  5  0 -1 -1 -1 -1

-1 -1 -1  0  5  0  5 -1 -1 -1 -1

-1 -1  0  5  0 -5  0  5  0 -1 -1

-1  0  5  0  0  0  0  0  5 -1 -1

-1  0  5  5  8  8  8  5  5 -1 -1

 0  5  5  0  0  0  0  0  5  5  0

 0  0 -1 -1 -1 -1 -1 -1 -1  0  0

-1 -1 -1 -1 -5 -5 -5 -1 -1 -1 -1
```

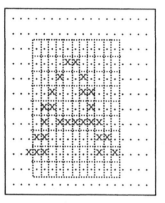

The templates are superimposed on the digitized image at the approximate location where the picture of a letter or a digit is found and the "fit ratio" is computed for each template. The template that gives the best fit determines the recognition result.

In the following structure Templ, the data member tag is the ASCII character represented by this template and the apmatrix<double> weights represents the weights for calculating the fit ratio.

```
struct Templ
{
    char tag;
    apmatrix<double> weights;
};
```

If t is a template, t.weights.numrows() and t.weights.numcols() return the dimensions of the template.

An image of a document is represented by the class `Image`, partially defined below:

```
class Image
{
  public:
    Image(istream & inFile);
      // Constructor: loads image data from a file

    void LocateChar(int & row, int & col) const;
      // Sets row and col to the approximate location of
      //   the upper left corner of the picture
      //   of the character in this image

    double FitRatio(const Templ & t, int row, int col) const;
      // Returns the fit ratio for a given template
      //   superimposed on this image at the (row,col)
      //   position

    < Other functions not shown >

  private:
    apmatrix<int> myPixels;
};
```

For testing purposes let us assume that a black-and-white image is stored in a text file in the following format. The first line holds the number of rows and columns in the image. The subsequent lines contain all the pixels, with black pixels represented as `'x'` and white pixels as `'.'`. For example:

```
12 18
..................
..................
..................
.......xx.........
......x..x........
.....x...xx.......
....xx....x.......
....x.xxxxxx......
...xx......xx.....
..xxx......x.x....
..................
..................
```

(a)   Write the constructor for the `Image` class, as started below:

```
Image::Image(istream & inFile)
// precondition:  inFile is a text file in the specified format,
//                open for reading.
// postcondition: The dimensions of the image are read from
//                the first line in inFile and myPixels is
//                resized accordingly.  Pixel data is read
//                from inFile and each element in myPixels
//                is set to 0 for a white pixel and 1 for
//                a black pixel read.
```

(b)   Write the member function `FitRatio` for the `Image` class. The function calculates the fit ratio for a given template placed over the image at a given position. The fit ratio is computed by multiplying the value (0 or 1) of each pixel in the image covered by the template by the corresponding weight and adding all the results. For a template of size 9 by 11, for example, 99 individual products contribute to the sum. The sum is then divided by the total number of pixels covered by the template and that number is returned as the fit ratio. (In the "real world" the template may be shifted in all directions slightly to obtain a better fit. Here, for the sake of simplicity, we examine just one position of the template.)

Complete the `FitRatio` function below the given header:

```
double Image::FitRatio(const Templ & t, int row, int col) const
// precondition:  row and col define the position
//                of the template -- the upper left corner.
//                The entire template at that position remains
//                within the boundaries of the image.
// postcondition: Returns the fit ratio for the template
//                placed at the (row, col) position.
//                The fit ratio is a weighted sum for all
//                pixels in the image covered by the template,
//                divided by the number of pixels in the
//                template.
```

(c) Write a function OCR as started below. Given an array of templates that represent a font and an image file opened for reading, this function returns the recognition result for the letter or digit in the image. The function returns '?' if none of the templates produces a positive fit ratio. Assume that a member function LocateChar is provided as described in the Image class definition, and that the constructor and the member function FitRatio work as specified, regardless of what you wrote in Parts (a) and (b).

```
char OCR(istream & inFile, const apvector<Templ> & font)
// precondition:  inFile has an image in the specified format
//                and is open for reading.
//                font contains font.length() templates.
// postcondition: Returns a character that corresponds to the
//                best-fitting template from the font or '?'
//                if none of the templates produces a positive
//                fit.
```

4.   This question refers to the *Case Study*. It can be found at

http://www.skylit.com/beprepared/a2fr.html

COMPUTER SCIENCE AB
SECTION I

Time — 1 hour and 15 minutes
Number of questions — 40
Percent of total grade — 50

1. In the following program segment, which assignment statement can never happen?

```
if (x <= y)
    a = 1;
else if (y < z)
    a = 2;
else if (x > z)
    a = 3;
else
    a = 4;
```

(A) `a = 1;`
(B) `a = 2;`
(C) `a = 3;`
(D) `a = 4;`
(E) Any one of the four assignments can happen

2. Assuming that x and y are Boolean variables, the expression

```
(x && !y) || (!x && y)
```

is equivalent to which of the following?

    I.   `(!x || !y) && (x || y)`
    II. `x != y`
    III. `(!x || y) && (x || !y)`

(A) I only
(B) II only
(C) III only
(D) I and II
(E) II and III

3.   What output does the following program produce?

```
void First(int & a, int & b)
{
    a++;
    b++;
}

int main()
{
    int num = 3;
    First (num, num);
    cout << num << endl;
    return 0;
}
```

(A)   3
(B)   4
(C)   5
(D)   6
(E)   Error message

4.   At the County Fair, prizes are awarded to the 5 heaviest pigs. There are more than 1000 pigs entered and their records are stored in an array. Which of these would be the most efficient way of finding the records of the 5 heaviest pigs?

(A)   Selection Sort
(B)   Selection Sort terminated after the first 5 iterations
(C)   Insertion Sort
(D)   Insertion Sort terminated after the first 5 iterations
(E)   Quicksort

Questions 5-6 use the following information. Suppose the * operator is overloaded for `apvector<double>` arguments, as follows:

```
double operator* (const apvector<double> & v1,
                  const apvector<double> & v2)
// postcondition: Returns the scalar product of v1 and v2.
{
    double sum = 0.0;
    int k;

    for (k = 0; k < v1.length() && k < v2.length(); k++)
        sum += v1[k] * v2[k];
    return sum;
}
```

5. If `x` is a variable of the `apvector<double>` type in a client program and `x.length() > 0`, what may be the result of the statement

    ```
    cout << (x*x);
    ```

   (A) An error due to undefined `operator* (apvector<double>)`
   (B) An error due to undefined `operator<< (apvector<double>)`
   (C) The program compiles and runs without errors; the output is never negative but may be zero when `x` contains all zeroes.
   (D) The program compiles and runs without errors; the output is always zero.
   (E) The program compiles without errors but gives a run-time subscript-out-of-bounds error when `x.length()` is 1.

6. You may not know it, but if `M` is an `apmatrix`, then `M[k]` refers to an `apvector` — the *k*-th row of `M`. Consider the following function:

    ```
    bool PropertyX (const apmatrix<double> & M)
    {
        int r1, r2, c;
        bool ok = true;

        for (r1 = 1; r1 < M.numrows(); r1++)
            for (r2 = 0; r2 < r1; r2++)
                ok = ok && (M[r1] * M[r2] == 0.);

        return ok;
    }
    ```

   `PropertyX` returns `true` if and only if

   (A) For any two different rows in `M` their scalar product is 0
   (B) For any two different rows in `M` their scalar product is not 0
   (C) The scalar product of the last row and any other row in `M` is not equal to 0
   (D) The scalar product of the last two rows in `M` is not equal to 0
   (E) The number of rows in `M` is 0

7. Consider the following code for a function that approximates the square root of a non-negative number:

```
double SquareRoot(double x)
{
    double x1 = 1, x2 = x;

    do
    {
        x2 = (x1 + x2) / 2;
        < statement >
    } while (fabs(x1 - x2) > 0.001);

    return x2;
}
```

What statement should replace < *statement* > so that the loop invariant is "x1 times x2 is equal to x" ?

(A) x1 = (x1 + x2) / 2;
(B) x1 = (x + x2) / 2;
(C) x1 = (x1 + x) / 2;
(D) x1 = x / x2;
(E) x1 = x / 2;

8. Consider two different designs for a data structure to hold the total number of home runs hit in a season by baseball players. There are *n* players, and each total is in the range 0 to 80.

    Design 1: Use an array of length 81. Each index into the array corresponds to a number of home runs and each element of the array is a pointer to a linked list containing the names of the players who hit that many home runs.

    Design 2: Use an array of length *n* so that each element of the array corresponds to one player. Each element of the array is a structure that contains the name of the player and the number of home runs hit by that player. The elements of the array are sorted alphabetically by player's name.

    This data structure will be used to support three operations:

    Operation 1: Given a player's name, look up that player's home run total.

    Operation 2: Given the names of two players, determine whether they hit the same number of home runs.

    Operation 3: Print the names of all players who hit over 50 home runs.

    Which of the three operations could be performed more efficiently using Design 1 rather than Design 2?

    (A) Operation 1 only
    (B) Operation 2 only
    (C) Operation 3 only
    (D) Operations 1 and 2
    (E) Operations 2 and 3

9. In a certain card game, cards are distributed into seven separate piles. The rules of the game permit moving several cards from the top of one pile onto the top of another pile without changing their order. Which of the following would be appropriate to simulate this aspect of the game without using additional data structures?

        I.   Seven linked lists
        II. Seven queues
        III. Seven stacks

    (A) I only
    (B) II only
    (C) III only
    (D) Either I or II
    (E) Either II or III

10. Suppose `Fun2` is defined as follows:

```
void Fun2(int x, int & y)
{
    y -= x;
}
```

What is the output from the following code?

```
int a = 3, b = 7;
Fun2(a, b);
Fun2(b, a);
cout << a << ' ' << b << endl;
```

(A)   3 7
(B)   3 4
(C)   -4 7
(D)   -1 4
(E)   -4 4

11. Assuming that p and q are variables of the type `double`, which of the following three code segments are equivalent (i.e., produce the same output for any values of p and q)?

I.
```
while (p > q)
{
    while (p > q)
    {
        cout << p;
        q++;
    }
    p--;
}
```

II.
```
while (p > q)
{
    if (p > q)
    {
        cout << p;
        q++;
    }
    p--;
}
```

III.
```
if (p > q)
{
    while (p > q)
    {
        cout << p;
        q++;
    }
    p--;
}
```

(A)   I and II
(B)   II and III
(C)   I and III
(D)   I, II, and III
(E)   All three are different

Questions 12-13 are based on the following function, which searches an array and returns the location of a target value item, if found, and -1 if not found. The array does not contain duplicate values and is sorted in ascending order.

```
int Search(const apvector<int> & A, int item)
{
    int first = 0, last = A.length() - 1;
    int middle;
    int targetPos = -1;

    while (first <= last && targetPos == -1)
    {
        middle = (first + last) / 2;
        if (item == A[middle])
            targetPos = middle;
        else if (item < A[middle])
            last = middle - 1;
        else
            first = middle + 1;
    }
    return targetPos;
}
```

12. How many times will the function run through the `while` loop if the array contains 20 elements and `A[19]` contains a value equal to `item`?

    (A) 1
    (B) 3
    (C) 4
    (D) 5
    (E) 6

13. Which of the following will be true after each pass through the `while` loop?

    (A) `item` equals `A[middle]` or `targetPos` equals -1
    (B) `item` equals `A[middle]` and `targetPos` does not equal -1
    (C) `first <= middle <= last`
    (D) `first < last`
    (E) None of the above

14. Suppose a program represents big non-negative integers as strings of decimal digits, '0' through '9', without leading zeroes. The most significant digit is the first character in the string. Consider the following incomplete code for the function LessThan:

```
bool LessThan(const apstring & bignum1,
              const apstring & bignum2)
// postcondition: Returns true if bignum1 is less than bignum2,
//                otherwise returns false.
{
    int len1 = bignum1.length(), len2 = bignum2.length();

    if (len1 < len2)
        return true;
    else if (len1 > len2)
        return false;

    < code >
}
```

Which of the following code segments can replace < *code* > so that the function works as specified?

I.   ```
return bignum1 < bignum2;
```

II.   ```
int k;
for (k = 0; k < len1; k++)
    if (bignum1[k] != bignum2[k])
        return (bignum1[k] < bignum2[k]);
return false;
```

III. ```
int k = 0;
while (k < len1 && bignum1[k] == bignum2[k])
    k++;
return (k < len1 && bignum1[k] < bignum2[k]);
```

(A)  I only
(B)  II only
(C)  III only
(D)  II and III
(E)  I, II, and III
```

15. What does the following function do?

```
double Something(const apmatrix<double> & M, int c)
// Precondition:  M is a square matrix.
{
    double sum = 0.0;
    int rows = M.numrows();
    int r;

    for (r = 0; r < rows; r++)
        sum += M[r][c];
    return sum;
}
```

(A)   Returns the sum of all the elements in a specified row of the matrix
(B)   Returns the sum of all the elements in a specified column of the matrix
(C)   Returns the sum of all the elements in one diagonal of the matrix
(D)   Returns the sum of all the elements in the matrix
(E)   Returns the sum of all the elements in the upper triangle of the matrix

16. Consider the following function:

```cpp
void PrintStars(const apvector<int> & list)
{
    int j, k;
    int len = list.length();

    for (j = 0; j < len; j++)
    {
        cout << j << ' ';
        if (list[j] % 2 == 0)
        {
            for (k = 0; k < list[j]; k++)
                cout << '*';
        }
        cout << endl;
    }
}
```

Given an apvector<int> A of length 5 containing values 3 4 5 0 1, what is the output when PrintStars(A) is called?

(A)   0 *
      1
      2 ***
      3
      4 *****

(B)   0 ***
      1
      2 *****
      3
      4 *

(C)   0
      1 ****
      2
      3
      4

(D)   3 *
      4
      5 ***
      0
      1 *****

(E)   3 ***
      4
      5 *****
      0
      1 *

17. Which of the following sorting algorithms, if any, requires, on average, $O(n^2)$ computational steps?

    (A)   Quicksort
    (B)   Mergesort
    (C)   Selection Sort
    (D)   Heapsort
    (E)   None of the above

Questions 18-21 use the following definitions:

```
struct Node
{
    char letter;
    Node * next;

    Node(char ch, Node * nx);   // Constructor
};

Node::Node(char ch, Node * nx)
  : letter(ch), next(nx)
{}

class List
{
  public:
    List();
    bool IsEmpty() const; // Returns true if the list is empty
    void Insert(char ch); // Inserts ch into the list
    bool Remove(char ch); // Removes the first node containing
                          //    ch from the list
    void Shuffle();       // Rearranges nodes in the list
    void Display() const; // Displays the list
    int Count() const;    // Returns the number of nodes

  private:
    Node * myHead;
};

List::List()
  : myHead(NULL)
{}
```

18. Suppose we plan to implement the List class by first coding and testing the constructor and two other member functions. Which pair of functions can be conveniently chosen to be developed and tested first?

    (A)   Insert and Display
    (B)   Display and Count
    (C)   Insert and Remove
    (D)   Shuffle and Remove
    (E)   Shuffle and Insert

19. Suppose `Insert` is implemented as follows:

```
void List::Insert(char ch)
{
    myHead = new Node(ch, myHead);
}
```

Which picture best describes the contents of the list `L` after the following segment of code is executed?

```
List L;
L.Insert('C');
L.Insert('H');
L.Insert('E');
```

(A)

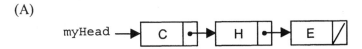

(B)

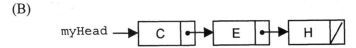

(C)

(D)

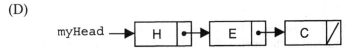

(E)   None of the above

20. Suppose `Remove` is implemented as follows:

```
bool List::Remove(char ch)
// postcondition: The node that contains the first
//                occurrence of ch is removed from the list.
//                Returns true if such a node is found, false
//                otherwise.
{
    if (IsEmpty())
        return false;
    else
    {
        Node * prev = NULL;
        Node * curr = myHead;
        while (curr != NULL && curr->letter != ch)
        {
            prev = curr;
            curr = curr->next;
        }
        prev->next = curr->next;
        delete curr;
        return true;
    }
}
```

When does the function `Remove` work correctly?

(A)   When `ch` is in the first but not in the last node of the list
(B)   When `ch` is in the last but not in the first node of the list
(C)   When `ch` is not found in any node of the list
(D)   When `ch` is in the only node of the list
(E)   Never

21. What does the following function Shuffle do?

```
void List::Shuffle()
{
    Node * s = myHead;
    Node * r = NULL;
    Node * p = NULL;

    while (s != NULL)
    {
        r = s->next;
        s->next = p;
        p = s;
        s = r;
    }
    myHead = p;
}
```

(A)   Unlinks the first node from the list
(B)   Unlinks all but the last node from the list
(C)   Unlinks the last node from the list
(D)   Leaves the list unchanged
(E)   Reverses the order of the nodes in the list

22. Suppose an empty stack is provided and an input stream contains the numbers
1 2 3 4 5 6, in this order. The numbers are read one by one from the input stream and either go directly into the output stream or are pushed onto the stack. When all the numbers from the input stream are processed, all the numbers from the stack are popped one by one and sent to the same output stream. Which of the following output streams would NOT be possible?

(A)   1 2 3 4 5 6
(B)   1 2 3 6 5 4
(C)   2 4 6 5 3 1
(D)   4 5 6 3 2 1
(E)   3 2 1 4 5 6

23. Consider designing a data structure for keeping track of student absences from school. Two methods are being considered:

   Method A: An array indexed by the days of the school year. Each element in the array is an `apvector` containing the names of absentees for the corresponding day in alphabetical order.

   Method B: An array of student records arranged in alphabetical order by student name. Each record contains a pointer to that student's list of absence dates sorted by date in ascending order.

   The following operations are to be implemented:

   Operation 1: List alphabetically all students with perfect attendance.
   Operation 2: List all days of the year that had at least 30% more absentees than average.

   Which of the following is true?

   (A)   Operation 1 can be implemented more efficiently using Method A; Operation 2 can be implemented more efficiently using Method B.
   (B)   Operation 1 can be implemented more efficiently using Method B; Operation 2 can be implemented more efficiently using Method A.
   (C)   Both Operation 1 and Operation 2 can be implemented more efficiently using Method A than using Method B.
   (D)   Both Operation 1 and Operation 2 can be implemented more efficiently using Method B than using Method A.
   (E)   Both Operation 1 and Operation 2 can be implemented equally efficiently using either method.

24. Which of the following values in an array can be a representation of a heap with the root value 5?

   I.   5 1 2 3 4
   II.   5 4 3 2 1
   III. 5 4 1 2 3

   (A)   I only
   (B)   II only
   (C)   III only
   (D)   II and III
   (E)   I, II, and III

25. The average time requirement of a Binary Search in an ordered array of size n is

   (A) $O(n/2)$
   (B) $O(n)$
   (C) $O(\log n)$
   (D) $O(n \log n)$
   (E) $O(n^2)$

26. Consider implementing a hash function, called Hash, for a hash table of size n, containing strings. Which of the following should be true of the value returned by the call Hash("fran")?

(A) The value should be 4 (the number of letters in the string).
(B) The value should be less than the value returned by the call Hash("gail"), since "fran" comes before "gail" in alphabetical order.
(C) The value should be the same as the value returned by the call Hash("ranf"), since these two strings contain the same characters.
(D) The value should be a prime number.
(E) The value should be in the range from 0 to n-1.

In Questions 27-28 consider the task of rearranging the elements in array A of n integers in such a way that all the negative numbers come before the non-negative numbers. The following algorithm is used:

```
Set left to the index of the first element
Set right to the index of the last element
while (left < right)
      while A[left] is negative, increment left
      while A[right] is non-negative, decrement right
      Swap A[left] with A[right], increment left, and decrement right
```

27. Under which of the following circumstances will the above algorithm result in an error?

I. When all the elements in the array are negative numbers.
II. When all the elements in the array are non-negative numbers.
III. When the array contains both negative and non-negative numbers sorted in ascending order.

(A) I only
(B) II only
(C) III only
(D) I and II
(E) I, II, and III

28. Which of the following best describes the running time of this algorithm (when it works correctly)?

(A) $O(n)$
(B) $O(n^2)$
(C) $O(\log n)$
(D) $O(n \log n)$
(E) Depends on the values in the array

29. A hash table resolves collisions through chaining, with individual buckets implemented as linked lists. If the table contains n items and best-case retrieval time is $O(1)$, which of the following may be the worst-case retrieval time?

    (A) $O(1)$
    (B) $O(\log n)$
    (C) $O(n)$
    (D) $O(n \log n)$
    (E) $O(n^2)$

30. Consider the following function:

```
void Change(apstack<int> & S, int n)
// precondition: 0 <= n <= S.length()
{
    int value;
    int k;
    apqueue<int> Q;

    for (k = 0; k < n; k++)
    {
        S.pop(value);
        Q.enqueue(value);
    }

    while (!Q.isEmpty())
    {
        Q.dequeue(value);
        S.push(value);
    }
}
```

Suppose a stack S contains the elements 1, 2, 3, 4, 5, with 5 being the top. What are the contents of S after the following code is executed?

```
int k;
for (k = 4; k > 0; k--)
{
    Change(S, k);
}
```

                $< top >$
                  ↓
    (A)   1 2 3 4 5
    (B)   1 5 4 3 2
    (C)   1 5 2 3 4
    (D)   1 5 3 2 4
    (E)   1 5 2 4 3

31. An *n* by *n* "magic square" contains consecutive integers 1, ..., n^2, arranged in such a way that the sum of each row, each column, and each diagonal is $n(n^2+1) / 2$. Consider the following code to check if a square, represented by an apmatrix, is magic.

```
bool IsMagic (const apmatrix<int> & M)
// precondition:  M is a square (n x n) matrix containing the
//                consecutive integers 1 ... n^2.
// postcondition: Returns true if the sum of each row,
//                column and diagonal is n(n^2 + 1) / 2.
{
    int row, col, sum;
    int n = M.numrows();
    int expectedSum = n*(n*n + 1)/2;

    for (row = 0; row < n; row++)
    {
        sum = 0;
        for (col = 0; col < n; col++)
            sum += M[row][col];
        if (sum != expectedSum)
            return false;
    }

    for (col = 0; col < n; col++)
    {
        sum = 0;
        for (row = 0; row < n; row++)
            sum += M[row][col];
        if (sum != expectedSum)
            return false;
    }

    sum = 0;
    for (row = 0; row < n; row++)
        sum += M[row][row];
    if (sum != expectedSum)
        return false;

    sum = 0;
    for (col = n - 1; col >= 0; col--)
        sum += M[col][col];
    if (sum != expectedSum)
        return false;

    return true;
}
```

In which of the following situations does the function return a WRONG value?

(A)   One row does not equal the expected sum
(B)   One column does not equal the expected sum
(C)   The diagonal from M[0][0] to M[n-1][n-1] does not equal the expected sum
(D)   The diagonal from M[0][n-1] to M[n-1][0] does not equal the expected sum
(E)   Never

32. Let us call a property of binary trees "inherited" if each of the subtrees has the property whenever the tree itself does. Which of the following is an "inherited" property for binary trees?

    (A)   Having an odd number of nodes
    (B)   Having an even number of nodes
    (C)   Having the same number of nodes in the left and right subtrees
    (D)   Having as many leaves as non-leaves
    (E)   Having no node with exactly one child

Questions 33-36 use the following definitions for a node of a binary tree:

```
struct TreeNode
{
    char info;
    TreeNode * left;
    TreeNode * right;
};
```

33. Which of the following is an appropriate postcondition for the following function?

```
TreeNode * FindNode(TreeNode * T)
// precondition:  T points to the root of a non-empty binary
//                search tree with non-empty left and right
//                subtrees.
// postcondition: <...>
{
    TreeNode * p = T->left;
    while (p->right != NULL)
    {
        p = p->right;
    }
    return p;
}
```

    (A)   Returns a pointer to the node containing the smallest value in T's right subtree.
    (B)   Returns a pointer to the node containing the largest value in T's left subtree.
    (C)   Returns a pointer to the node containing the largest value in the tree.
    (D)   Returns a pointer to the rightmost node on the level farthest from the root.
    (E)   Returns a pointer to the rightmost leaf in the tree.

34. Consider the following function:

```
bool Check(TreeNode * T)
{
    if (T == NULL)
        return false;
    return ((T->left != NULL) && (T->right != NULL)) ||
            Check(T->left) ||
            Check(T->right);
}
```

This function returns `true` if and only if the tree pointed to by `T`

(A)   is not empty
(B)   has at least one node with two children
(C)   is not empty and the root is not a leaf
(D)   is not empty and each node is either a leaf or has two children
(E)   is a full tree

35. Consider the following function:

```
void Manipulate(TreeNode * T)
{
    TreeNode * temp;
    if (T != NULL)
    {
        temp = T->right;
        T->right = T->left;
        T->left = temp;
        Manipulate(T ->left);
        Manipulate(T ->right);
    }
}
```

What is the result when the function Manipulate is applied to the following tree?

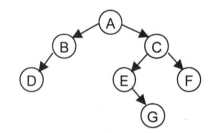

(A)

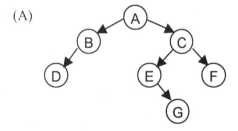

(B)

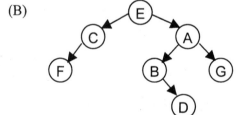

(C)

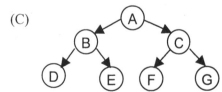

(D)

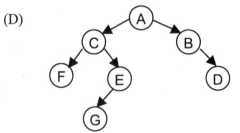

(E)

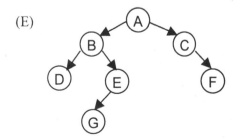

36. Suppose the following binary search tree was constructed by inserting nodes, one at a time:

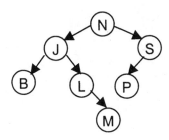

The algorithm used inserts a new node as a leaf. Which of the following could NOT be the sequence in which the nodes were inserted?

(A)   N J B L M S P
(B)   N S P J L M B
(C)   N L M J B S P
(D)   N J L B S M P
(E)   N J S L P M B

<u>Questions 37-40</u> refer to the *Case Study*. These questions can be found at:

    http://www.skylit.com/beprepared/ab1mc.html

COMPUTER SCIENCE AB
SECTION II

Time — 1 hour and 45 minutes
Number of questions — 4
Percent of total grade — 50

1. A two-dimensional black-and-white screen is represented by the class `Screen` partially
    defined below. The constructor is also shown. Each element in the `apmatrix myPixels`
    represents one pixel on the screen. A blank screen is represented by an array that contains
    all `Screen::white` values.

```
class Screen
{
  public:
    enum Color {white, black};   // Legal pixel values
    Screen (int rows, int cols); // Constructor: builds
                                 //   a blank (white) screen
                                 //   of the given size
    int numrows() const;         // Returns number of rows
    int numcols() const;         // Returns number of columns
    bool IsBlank(int row, int col) const;
                                 // Returns true if the pixel
                                 //   at row, col is white and
                                 //   false otherwise
    void ChangeColor(int row, int col);
                                 // Changes the color of the
                                 //   pixel at row, col

  private:
    int myNumrows;
    int myNumcols;
    apmatrix<Color> myPixels;
};

Screen::Screen (int rows, int cols)
  : myNumrows(rows), myNumcols(cols),
                  myPixels(rows, cols, Screen::white)
  {}
```

(a) Write a public member function that, given the coordinates of a pixel, will change the color of the pixel. For example, given a screen shown below, the call ChangeColor(3,4) will change the black pixel in row 3 and column 4 to white; the call ChangeColor(0,1) will turn the pixel in row 0 and column 1 to black.

You can assume that the function IsBlank works as specified.

```
void Screen::ChangeColor(int row, int col)
// precondition:  0 <= row < myNumrows; 0 <= col < myNumcols
// postcondition: The color of the pixel at row, col position
//                is changed from white to black or from black
//                to white.
```

(b)   Write a function `Magnetize`, as started below. The function moves all the black pixels on a given screen one position closer to a given pixel, a "magnet." You will write only a particular case of `Magnetize` when the magnet is the pixel in the upper right corner of the screen. The function moves a black pixel that shares a row or a column with the magnet by one square closer to the magnet in that row or that column respectively. A black pixel that does not share a row or a column with the magnet moves diagonally by one square in the direction of the magnet. If the magnet pixel happens to be black, it remains unchanged. Black pixels may merge in the same destination. For example:

Before: After `Magnetize(S)`:

Assume that `ChangeColor` works as specified regardless of what you wrote in Part (a).

```
void Magnetize(Screen & S)
// precondition:  S is initialized with black and white pixels.
// postcondition: Each black pixel is moved one space
//                in the same row, column, or diagonally
//                toward the upper right corner.
```

(c)   Write an overloaded + operator for `Screen` objects. The operator builds a new `Screen` object from two given screens, its operands, as stated in the precondition and postcondition below. Assume that `ChangeColor` works as specified regardless of what you wrote in Part (a).

```
Screen operator+ (const Screen & s1, const Screen & s2)
// precondition:  s1 and s2 have the same dimensions.
// postcondition: Returns a new screen that has the same
//                dimensions as s1 and s2.  The new screen has
//                a black pixel in a particular position
//                if and only if either s1 or s2 or both
//                have black pixels in that position.
```

2. In the early days of computing, punch cards were used to store data. Sorting of data actually involved bins for the cards.

Consider the following sorting method, called the Radix Sort. Suppose you had 12 integers in the range from 0 to 999, each represented on one punch card. For example:

```
23 386 993 976 154 294 91 396 634 2 11 70
```

The machine would use 10 bins, 0 through 9. First all the numbers (punch cards) would be scanned in order and placed in the bins according to their ones digit. The 23 would be placed in the 3 bin, the 386 in the 6 bin, and so on:

[0]	[1]	[2]	[3]	[4]	[5]	[6]	[7]	[8]	[9]
70	91	2	23	154		386			
	11		993	294		976			
				634		396			

Then the cards would be gathered up from bins in order and the list would become

```
70 91 11 2 23 993 154 294 634 386 976 396
```

The next time, the cards would be placed in the bins according to their tens digit. So 70 would be placed in the 7 bin, and so on:

[0]	[1]	[2]	[3]	[4]	[5]	[6]	[7]	[8]	[9]
2	11	23	634		154		70	386	91
							976		993
									294
									396

Then the cards would be gathered up from the bins again and the list would become

```
2 11 23 634 154 70 976 386 91 993 294 396
```

The final time, the cards would be placed in the bins according to their hundreds digit:

[0]	[1]	[2]	[3]	[4]	[5]	[6]	[7]	[8]	[9]
2	154	294	386			634			976
11			396						993
23									
70									
91									

When the cards were gathered for the third time, the machine would end up with the list sorted in ascending order. The required number of iterations would be the number of digits in the largest number.

The RadixSort class below implements this sorting method for sorting a linked list of numbers using bins also implemented as linked lists. The implementation is also shown for the constructor, the Sort member function, and the Distribute member function that distributes nodes from a list into bins.

```
struct Node
{
    int value;
    Node * next;
};

void Append(Node * & list1, Node * list2);
     // Appends list2 at the end of list1

Node * Unlink (Node * & list);
     // Unlinks the first node from a given list and returns a
     //    pointer to it

const int MAX_DIGITS = < max number of digits in numbers > ;

class RadixSort
{
  public:
    RadixSort();
    void Sort(Node * & list);

  private:
    apvector<Node *> myBins;
                        // Array of pointers to 10 bins
    void Distribute(Node * & list, int d);
                        // Distributes nodes from list into bins,
                        //    according to their d-th digit
    Node * Gather();    // Returns a pointer to the combined
                        //    list, gathered from bins
    int WhatBin(int value, int d);
                        // Returns the number of the bin (0-9)
                        //    to which value should be placed,
                        //    based on its d-th digit
};
```

```
RadixSort::RadixSort()   // Constructor
  : myBins(10, NULL)
{}

void RadixSort::Sort(Node * &list)
// precondition:  list points to a list of elements.
//                All bins are empty.
// postcondition: The elements of list are sorted in ascending
//                order.  All bins are empty.
{
    int d;
    for (d = 1; d <= MAX_DIGITS; d++)
    {
        Distribute(list, d);
        list = Gather();
    }
}

void RadixSort::Distribute (Node * & list, int d)
// precondition:  list points to a list of elements.
//                All bins are empty.
// postcondition: The elements from list are distributed
//                into bins according to their d-th digit.
{
    Node * temp;
    int bin;

    while (list != NULL)
    {
        temp = Unlink(list);
        bin = WhatBin(temp->value, d);
        Append(myBins[bin], temp);
    }
}
```

(a) Write the function Unlink, as started below. This function separates the first node from list, updates list to point to the next node, converts the unlinked node into a one-node list, and returns a pointer to it.

```
Node * Unlink (Node * & list)
// precondition:  list points to a non-empty list of nodes.
// postcondition: The first node of list is removed from
//                list, list is updated to point to the next
//                node or NULL.  Returns a pointer to the
//                unlinked node after setting its data member
//                "next" to NULL.
```

(b) Write the function Append that appends the second list at the end of the first.

```
void Append (Node * & list1, Node * list2)
// precondition:  list1 and/or list2 are either empty (have
//                the value NULL) or point to linked lists.
// postcondition: list2 has been appended at the end of list1.
```

(c) Write the private member function Gather that gathers all the elements from myBins in order into one list and returns a pointer to that list, leaving myBins empty. In writing this function, you may use the function Append. Assume that this function works as specified regardless of what you wrote in Part (b).

```
Node * RadixSort::Gather()
// precondition:  myBins[0], ..., myBins[9] point to lists.
// postcondition: All elements from the lists pointed to
//                by myBins[bin] are gathered into one list.
//                Returns a pointer to the combined list.
//                myBins[0], ..., myBins[9] are left empty.
```

3.   Consider a binary tree, implemented as follows:

```
struct TreeNode
{
    char info;
    TreeNode * left;
    TreeNode * right;

    // Constructor:
    TreeNode (char ch, TreeNode * lc, TreeNode * rc);
};

TreeNode::TreeNode (char ch, TreeNode * lc, TreeNode * rc)
   : info(ch), left(lc), right(rc)
{}
```

(a) Let us call the *height* of a tree the length of the longest path from the root node to a leaf. For example, a tree with only one node has a height of 0 and the tree illustrated below has a height of 3.

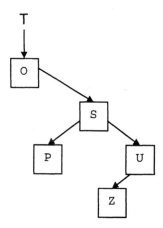

Write a function `Height` as started below. In writing your function you may call the function `Max(a,b)` which returns the larger of two integers.

```
int Height(TreeNode * T)
// precondition:  T is either NULL or points to
//                a binary tree.
// postcondition: If T is NULL returns -1,
//                otherwise returns the height of
//                the tree pointed to by T.
```

(b) Write a function `AddSiblings` that takes a binary tree and adds to all nodes with only one child another child containing a given value. For example:

<u>Before</u>   <u>After the call to `AddSiblings(T, 'X')`</u>

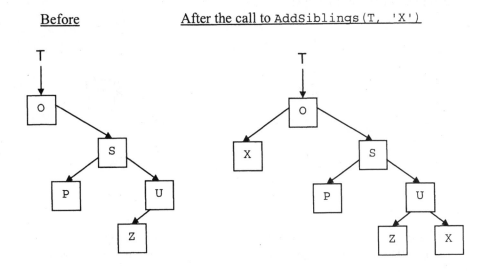

```
void AddSiblings (TreeNode * T, char ch)
// precondition:  T is NULL or points to the root of a
//                binary tree.
// postcondition: Another child with the value ch has been
//                added to each node in T that had exactly
//                one child.
```

(c) A binary tree is said to be *full* if all its levels are filled with nodes. A full tree contains the maximum possible number of nodes for a binary tree of a certain height. For example, these are full trees:

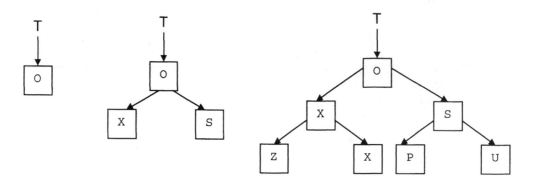

Write the function `IsFullTree` as started below. In writing this function you may assume that `Height` works as specified regardless of what you wrote in Part (a).

```
bool IsFullTree (TreeNode * T)
// precondition:   T points to a non-empty binary tree.
// postcondition: Returns true if T is a full tree,
//                false otherwise.
```

4.   This question refers to the *Case Study*. It can be found at

http://www.skylit.com/beprepared/ab1fr.html

COMPUTER SCIENCE AB
SECTION I

Time — 1 hour and 15 minutes
Number of questions — 40
Percent of total grade — 50

1. What output is produced by the following program?

```
#include <iostream.h>

void Process(int a, int & b)
{
    a *= a;
    b *= a;
}

int main()
{
    int m = 2, n = 2;

    Process(m, n);
    cout << m << n << endl;
    return 0;
}
```

(A) 42
(B) 24
(C) 48
(D) 28
(E) An error message

2.   Suppose Trick(x) is defined as follows:

```
char Trick(int & x)
{
    if (x < 0)
    {
        x = -x;
        return '-';
    }
    else
        return '+';
}
```

Assuming that apvector<int> V contains the values 0, -1, 2, -3, what is the output from the following code?

```
char s;
int k;
for (k = 0; k < 4; k++)
{
    s = Trick(V[k]);
    cout << s << V[3-k];
}
```

(A)   +3+2+1+0

(B)   -+3+2-+1+0

(C)   +-3-2+-1-0

(D)   +-3-2+1-0

(E)   --3+2--1+0

3.   Consider the following function:

```
double SumTopTwo(const apvector<double> & A)
// precondition:  A.length() >= 2; A is filled with random
//                   values.
// postcondition: Returns the largest sum of two elements in A.
{
    int len = A.length();
    int k, k1 = 0, k2 = 1;

    for (k = 2; k < len; k++)
    {
        if (A[k] > A[k1])
        {
            k2 = k1;
            k1 = k;
        }
        else if (A[k] > A[k2])
            k2 = k;
    }
    return A[k1] + A[k2];
}
```

Which of the following best describes the condition under which SumTopTwo may fail to work as specified?

(A)   A[0] is less than A[1]
(B)   A has only two elements
(C)   A contains duplicate values
(D)   A contains both positive and negative values
(E)   A is sorted in descending order

4. The two versions of the function Search shown below are both intended to return true if array A contains the target value and false otherwise.

Version 1:

```
bool Search(const apvector<int> & A, int value)
{
    int k;
    for (k = 0; k < A.length(); k++)
    {
        if (A[k] == value)
            return true;
    }
    return false;
}
```

Version 2:

```
bool Search(const apvector<int> & A, int value)
{
    int k;
    bool found = false;
    for (k = 0; k < A.length(); k++)
    {
        if (A[k] == value)
            found = true;
    }
    return found;
}
```

Which of the following statements about the two versions of Search is true?

(A) Only Version 1 will work as intended.
(B) Only Version 2 will work as intended.
(C) Both versions will work as intended; Version 1 will often be more efficient than Version 2.
(D) Both versions will work as intended; Version 2 will often be more efficient than Version 1.
(E) Both versions will work as intended; the two versions will always be equally efficient.

5. Given that x is *true*, y is *true* and z is *false*, which of the following expressions will evaluate to *false*?

(A)   (x && y) || z
(B)   (x || y) && z
(C)   y || (x && z)
(D)   x || (y && z)
(E)   x && (y || z)

6. Suppose you wanted to write a function XOR (A, B) with two Boolean arguments. The function should return true if and only if exactly one of the arguments is true. Which of the following would calculate the appropriate return value?

```
I.    (A && !B) || (!A && B)
II.   A != B
III.  (A || B) && (!A || !B)
```

(A) I only
(B) II only
(C) III only
(D) II and III
(E) I, II, and III

7. Consider the following function:

```
void Copy2(const apstring & A, const apstring & B,
                apstring & C, apstring & D)
{
    C = A;
    D = B;
}
```

What is the output from the following code segment?

```
apstring X("Junior "), Y("Senior ");
Copy2(X, Y, Y, X);
cout << X << ' ' << Y;
```

(A) Senior Junior
(B) Junior Senior
(C) Senior Senior
(D) Junior Junior
(E) Junior Senior Junior Senior

8.   Consider the following function:

```
int Mystery(int m, int n)
// precondition:  m and n are non-negative integers.
// postcondition: <...>
{
    int count = 0;
    do
    {
        if (m % 10 == n)
            count++;
        m /= 10;
    } while (m > 0);

    return count;
}
```

Which of the following best describes what Mystery returns?

(A)   The number of times the digit n occurs in the decimal representation of m
(B)   The number of common digits in the corresponding places in m and n
(C)   The number of digits in m written in base n
(D)   The highest power of n that is below m
(E)   The greatest common factor of m and n

9.   apmatrix<int> S holds brightness values for pixels (picture elements) on a screen. The values range from 0 to 255. Consider the following function:

```
int FindMax(const apmatrix<int> & S)
{
    apvector<int> count(256, 0);
    int r, c;
    int i, iMax = 0;

    for (r = 0; r < S.numrows(); r++)
        for (c = 0; c < S.numcols(); c++)
        {
            i = S[r][c];
            count[i]++;
        }
    for (i = 1; i < 256; i++)
        if (count[i] > count[iMax])
            iMax = i;
    return iMax;
}
```

What does this function compute?

(A)   The column with the highest sum of brightness values in s
(B)   The maximum brightness value for all pixels in s
(C)   The most frequent brightness value in s
(D)   The maximum total sum of brightness values in any 256 consecutive rows in s
(E)   The maximum total sum of brightness values in any 256 by 256 square in s

Questions 10-13 are based on the class `Restaurant` partially defined below. The class describes the occupancy of tables in a restaurant and the costs of meal orders. A `Restaurant` object maintains an array (`apvector`) `myTables` with each table represented by the following structure:

```
struct Table
{
    int numDiners;
    apstring mealOrder;
    double mealCost;

    Table();
};

Table::Table()
   : numDiners(0), mealOrder(""), mealCost(0.0)
{}
```

It is assumed that all tables are the same size and have the same number of chairs:

```
const int TABLE_SIZE = 4;
```

```
class Restaurant
{
  public:
    Restaurant(int nTables);

    int Size();
    // postcondition: Returns the number of tables in
    //                the restaurant.

    void GetTable(int tbl, int p);
    // precondition:  0 <= tbl < myTables.length()
    //                Table tbl is empty;
    //                0 < p <= TABLE_SIZE
    // postcondition: p customers have been seated at table tbl.

    void PlaceOrder(int tbl);
    // precondition:  Table tbl is not empty.
    // postcondition: Food and drink have been ordered
    //                and the meal cost has been computed.

    int ShowOccupancy(int tbl);
    // precondition:  0 <= tbl < myTables.length()
    // postcondition: Returns the number of occupied chairs
    //                at table tbl.

    double ShowCost(int tbl);
    // precondition:  0 <= tbl < myTables.length()
    // postcondition: Returns the cost of the meal for
    //                table tbl.

    void VacateTable(int tbl);
    // precondition:  Table tbl is not empty.
    // postcondition: Itemized bill is displayed;
    //                table tbl is vacated.

    < Other functions not shown >

  private:
    apvector<Table> myTables;
    double myTotalReceipts;
};

Restaurant::Restaurant(int numTables)
  : myTables(numTables), myTotalReceipts(0.0)
{}
```

10. Suppose a programmer decided to code and test the constructor and two other member functions for the `Restaurant` class, temporarily commenting out other functions. Which of the following pairs of functions are the best candidates for being implemented and tested first?

    (A)   `GetTable` and `ShowOccupancy`
    (B)   `GetTable` and `VacateTable`
    (C)   `PlaceOrder` and `ShowOccupancy`
    (D)   `PlaceOrder` and `VacateTable`
    (E)   `GetTable` and `PlaceOrder`

11. Which of the following is the most appropriate replacement for < *message* > in the code segment below?

```
Restaurant Hotcakes(20);
...
int t, count = 0;
for (t = 0; t < Hotcakes.Size(); t++)
    count += Hotcakes.ShowOccupancy(t);
cout <<  < message >  << count << endl;
```

    (A)   `"The number of occupied tables is "`
    (B)   `"The current number of diners is "`
    (C)   `"The maximum numbers of diners per table is "`
    (D)   `"The maximum possible number of diners is "`
    (E)   `"The number of empty chairs is "`

12. Suppose the tables are numbered 0, 1, ..., in order of desirability of location with 0 being the best table. When a party enters the restaurant, they are seated at the most desirable empty table. The code segment below sits a party of 3 in the `Restaurant Hotcakes`:

```
int t = 0;
while (Hotcakes.ShowOccupancy(t) > 0)
    t++;
Hotcakes.GetTable(t, 3);
```

    In which of the following situations will this code fail to work properly?

    (A)   If and only if all tables are occupied
    (B)   If and only if all tables are empty
    (C)   If and only if all chairs are occupied
    (D)   Never
    (E)   Always

13. Which of the following code segments correctly calculates the average cost per meal for all the people currently dining in the Hotcakes restaurant, assuming that Hotcakes is not empty?

(A)
```
double avgCost = Hotcakes.ShowCost() / Hotcakes.ShowOccupancy();
```

(B)
```
double avgCost = Hotcakes.ShowCost() / TABLE_SIZE;
```

(C)
```
int t, count = 0;
double cost = 0.0;
for(t = 0; t < Hotcakes.Size(); t++)
{
    count += Hotcakes.ShowOccupancy(t);
    cost += Hotcakes.ShowCost(t);
}
double avgCost = cost / count;
```

(D)
```
int t;
double cost = 0.0;
for (t = 0; t < Hotcakes.Size(); t++)
    cost += Hotcakes.ShowCost(t);
double avgCost = cost / (Hotcakes.Size() * TABLE_SIZE);
```

(E)   None of the above

14. Consider the following function:

```
void Message(int n)
{
    if (n > 0)
        cout << '+';
    else
    {
        cout << '-';
        Message(n + 1);
    }
}
```

What is the output when Message(-1) is called?

(A)   ---+
(B)   --+
(C)   -+
(D)   ---
(E)   --+++++++... (-- followed by an infinite sequence of +'s)

15. Consider the function `Repeats` below.

```
bool Repeats(const apstring & str)
// postcondition: Returns true if any two consecutive characters
//                in str are the same, false otherwise.
{
    int k;
    for (k = 1; k < str.length(); k++)
    {
        if (str[0] == str[k])
            return true;
    }
    return false;
}
```

For which of the following strings will the function `Repeats` NOT work as specified?

(A)   `"away"`
(B)   `"aaaa"`
(C)   `"wxyz"`
(D)   `"aardvark"`
(E)   `"x"`

16. What is the result when the following code segment is executed?

```
apstring url = "http://www.usa.gov";

if (url.find("http://") != npos)
    cout << url.substr(7, url.length()-7);
else
    cout << "not found";
```

(A)   Compiler error "npos is not defined"
(B)   Runtime error "subscript out of range"
(C)   Displays `not found`
(D)   Displays `usa.gov`
(E)   Displays `www.usa.gov`

17. Consider the following structure with a constructor and a program that uses it:

```
struct Ladder
{
    int length;
    apvector<int> rungs;

    Ladder(int n, int step);   // Constructor
};

Ladder::Ladder(int n, int step)
{
    int i;
    for (i = 0; i < n; i++)
        rungs[i] = (i+1) * step;
    length = n;
}

int main()
{
    Ladder ld(5, 2);

    cout << (ld.rungs[0] + ld.rungs[1]) / 2 << endl;
    return 0;
}
```

What happens when this program is compiled and run?

(A)   The program fails to compile because the constructor doesn't have an initializer list.
(B)   The program fails to run because the structure Ladder doesn't have a default constructor.
(C)   The program compiles and runs with no errors and displays 1.
(D)   The program compiles and runs with no errors and displays 3.
(E)   The program compiles and runs, but it is aborted with a "subscript out of bounds" error.

Questions 18-19 refer to the following function:

```
int Product (int n)
{
    if (n <= 1)
        return 1;
    else
        return n * Product(n-2);
}
```

18. What is the output when Product(6) is called?

(A)   1
(B)   8
(C)   12
(D)   48
(E)   720

19. If you call the function `Product` with a positive argument and a negative integer is returned, what would most likely account for this result?

   (A)   Logic error that shows up for odd values of n
   (B)   Syntax error
   (C)   Compiler error
   (D)   Linker error
   (E)   Integer arithmetic overflow

20. The function below is supposed to count the number of negative integers in a queue, leaving the queue in its original state.

```
int CountNegs(apqueue<int> & q)
{
    int first, num, count = 0;
    if (q.isEmpty())
        return 0;
    q.dequeue(first);
    if (first < 0)
        count++;
    q.enqueue(first);

    while (q.front() != first)
    {
        q.dequeue(num);
        if (num < 0)
            count++;
        q.enqueue(num);
    }
    return count;
}
```

   This function does not always work correctly. Which of the following best characterizes a queue for which the function will return a wrong answer?

   (A)   An empty queue
   (B)   A queue that contains exactly one integer
   (C)   A queue that contains the same integer at the front and elsewhere in the queue
   (D)   A queue that contains an odd number of integers
   (E)   A queue that contains an even number of integers

21. Consider the following code segment where S is an apstack and Q is an apqueue:

```
int j, num;

for (j = 0; j < 6; j++)
{
    Q.dequeue(num);
    if (num % 2 == 1)
        S.push(j);
    else
        Q.enqueue(j);
}

while (!S.isEmpty())
{
    S.pop(num);
    cout << num << ' ';
}

while (!Q.isEmpty())
{
    Q.dequeue(num);
    cout << num << ' ';
}

cout << endl;
```

If Q has 6, 8, 7, 5, 12, and 16 stored in it (with 6 being the first element and 16 being the last), what is the output when the above code segment is executed?

(A)   3 2 0 1 4 5
(B)   5 4 1 0 2 3
(C)   5 7 6 8 12 16
(D)   0 1 4 5 3 2
(E)   16 12 8 6 7 5

Questions 22-23 are based on the following code:

```
const int limit = < Some value >;
apqueue<int> Q;
bool found;
int n = 2, k, d;

Q.enqueue(n);
while (n < limit)
{
    found = false;
    for (k = 0; k < Q.length(); k++)
    {
        Q.dequeue(d);
        if (n % d == 0)
            found = true;
        Q.enqueue(d);
    }
    if (!found)
        Q.enqueue(n);
    n++;
}

while (!Q.isEmpty())
{
    Q.dequeue(d);
    cout << d << ' ';
}
cout << endl;
```

22. What is the output from the above code segment if `limit` is 6?

    (A) 4 2
    (B) 5 4 3 2
    (C) 2 3 5
    (D) 2 3 4 5
    (E) 5 3 2

23. Which of the following can serve as a reasonable loop invariant for the loop
    `while (n < limit)`?

    (A) `found` is false if and only if `n % d != 0`
    (B) Q contains all the prime numbers less than or equal to n
    (C) Q contains all the integers from 2 to n
    (D) The number of elements in Q is less than `limit`
    (E) n is less than `limit`

24. What does it mean to have a collision in a hash table?

    (A)   The hash table becomes full
    (B)   The hash function returns a negative location
    (C)   Two different items that hash to the same location are inserted into the hash table
    (D)   The hash function returns a number larger than the size of the hash table
    (E)   The hash function is called more than once for the same item, so it returns the same result multiple times

25. The structure below represents a node of a doubly-linked list with links from each node to the previous and the next node.

```
struct Node
{
    apstring info;
    Node * prev;
    Node * next;
};
```

    Consider the following function:

```
void RemoveFromList(Node * p)
// precondition:  p points to one of the nodes in a
//                doubly-linked list that contains at least
//                three nodes.
// postcondition: The node pointed to by p is removed from
//                the list.
{
    p->prev->next = p->next;
    p->next->prev = p->prev;
    delete p;
}
```

    In which of the following cases will the RemoveFromList function work properly?

        I.   p points to the first node in the list.
        II.   p points to the second node in the list.
        III. p points to the last node in the list.

    (A)   II only
    (B)   I and II only
    (C)   I and III only
    (D)   II and III only
    (E)   I, II, and III

26. If a binary tree has 17 nodes, at most how many of them can be leaves?

    (A)   1
    (B)   8
    (C)   9
    (D)   16
    (E)   17

27. For which of the following binary trees does preorder traversal produce APCS and postorder traversal produce CPSA?

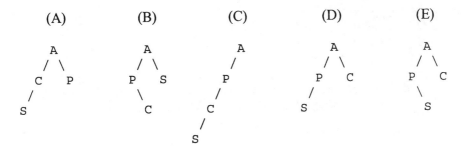

(A)   (B)   (C)   (D)   (E)

28. Suppose the nodes of a binary tree are represented by the following structure:

```
struct TreeNode
{
    char info;
    TreeNode * left;
    TreeNode * right;
};
```

Consider the following function:

```
bool CheckTree (TreeNode * T)
{
    if (T == NULL)
    {
        return false;
    }
    else
    {
        return (T->left != NULL && T->right == NULL) ||
               (T->left == NULL && T->right != NULL) ||
               CheckTree(T->left) ||
               CheckTree(T->right);
    }
}
```

CheckTree returns true if and only if the tree pointed to by T

(A)   is not empty
(B)   is not empty and the root is a leaf
(C)   is not empty and the root is either a leaf or has one child
(D)   has at least one node with one child
(E)   is a full tree

Questions 29-31 are based on the following class that implements a priority queue of integers. In this priority queue the value of an item is also used as the item's priority:

```
class PriorityQ
{
  public:

    PriorityQ();
      // Constructor: builds an empty priority queue with
      //   the capacity to hold 100 items

    void Insert(int item);
      // Inserts item into the priority queue

    int Serve();
      // Returns the highest-ranking item from the
      //   priority queue

  private:

    void ReheapUp();
      // Restores heap ordering in myLine with an
      //   element out of order in position myLength-1.

    void ReheapDown();
      // Restores heap ordering in myLine with an
      //   element out of order in position 0.

    int myLength;
      // The number of items in the priority queue

    apvector<int> myItems;
      // The array of items stored as a heap.
      // myItems[0] holds the root element of the heap.
};

void PriorityQ::Insert(int item)
// precondition:  myItems has room for at least one more item.
// postcondition: item is inserted into myItems, preserving
//                the heap ordering.
{
    myItems[myLength] = item;
    myLength++;
    ReheapUp();
}
```

```
void PriorityQ::ReheapUp()
// precondition:  The heap is empty or the element in the last
//                position in myItems may be out of order.
// postcondition: If necessary, myItems is reordered to satisfy
//                the heap ordering property.
{
    if (myLength == 0)
        return;

    int k = myLength-1;
    int hold = myItems[k];
    int parent;

    while (k > 0)
    {
        parent = (k-1)/2;
        if (hold < myItems[parent])
            break;
        myItems[k] = myItems[parent];
        k = parent;
    }
    myItems[k] = hold;
}
```

29. What will be the order of the elements in myItems after the following code fragment is executed?

```
PriorityQ line;
line.Insert(9);
line.Insert(1);
line.Insert(5);
line.Insert(6);
```

(A)   1, 6, 5, 9
(B)   9, 6, 5, 1
(C)   9, 5, 6, 1
(D)   9, 1, 5, 6
(E)   1, 5, 6, 9

30. Which of the following best describes the average running time for the Insert function when a random integer is inserted into a random priority queue with n elements?

(A) $O(1)$
(B) $O(n)$
(C) $O(n^2)$
(D) $O(\log n)$
(E) $O(n \log n)$

31. Under which of the following conditions will the function ReheapUp fail to work as specified?

    (A)   When the last element in myItems is the largest
    (B)   When the heap happens to be already in order
    (C)   When the queue is empty
    (D)   When the queue has one element in it
    (E)   Never

Questions 32-33 refer to a circular linked list. The nodes in such a list are arranged in a circular formation with each node having a pointer to the next node. If one node is designated as "first," then the "last" node points back to it. The list is addressed by a pointer to one of the nodes. Suppose the nodes of the list are represented using the following structure with a constructor:

```
struct Node
{
    apstring info;
    Node * next;

    Node (const apstring & str, Node * nx); // Constructor
};

Node::Node (const apstring & str, Node * nx)
    : info(str), next(nx)
{}
```

32. The function Print below has a missing condition in the do-while loop:

```
void Print (Node * start)
// precondition:   start points to a node of a non-empty
//                 circular list.
// postcondition: info data member from all nodes is printed
//                 to cout.
{
    Node * ptr = start;
    do
    {
        cout << ptr->info << endl;
        ptr = ptr->next;
    } while ( < condition > );
}
```

Which of the following is an appropriate replacement for < condition > ?

    (A)   ptr != NULL
    (B)   ptr != start
    (C)   ptr != start->next
    (D)   ptr->next != start
    (E)   ptr->next != start->next

33. Consider the following function:

```
void AddNode (Node * & start, const apstring & str)
// precondition:  start is either NULL, indicating an empty
//                list, or points to a node of a circular list.
// postcondition: A node containing str has been allocated and
//                added to the list.
{
    Node * temp = new Node(str, NULL);
    if (start == NULL)
    {
        start = temp;
        temp->next = temp;
    }
    else
    {
        < statement A >
        < statement B >
    }
}
```

Which of the following pairs of statements correctly completes this function?

	< statement A >	< statement B >
(A)	temp->next = start->next;	start->next = temp;
(B)	start->next = temp;	temp->next = start->next;
(C)	start->next = temp;	temp->next = start;
(D)	start = temp;	temp->next = start->next;
(E)	start = temp;	start->next = temp->next;

34. A master list of past contributors to a large charitable organization is maintained in alphabetical order. After each fundraising event, an unsorted relatively small list of new contributors has to be added to the master list. Which of the following sorting algorithms would be the most efficient algorithm for this task?

(A) Quicksort
(B) Heapsort
(C) Mergesort
(D) Insertion Sort
(E) Selection Sort

35. One task of a compiler is to check that each pair of delimiter symbols, such as braces or parentheses, match. In writing a parsing function that checks that pairs of braces match, which of the following ADTs would be most useful for temporarily saving the location of the opening brace until a matching closing brace is found?

(A) An array
(B) A linked list
(C) A stack
(D) A queue
(E) A binary search tree

36. A function CountNegatives returns the number of negative values in an array. The precondition is that all positive values, if any, follow all negative values, if any, in the array, and that the array does not contain any zeroes. The function works by comparing certain elements of the array to 0. If $t(n)$ is the number of comparisons that guarantees the correct result for any array of n elements, even in the worst case, what is $t(10)$ in an optimal algorithm?

    (A)   4
    (B)   5
    (C)   8
    (D)   9
    (E)   10

Questions 37-40 refer to the *Case Study*. These questions can be found at:

http://www.skylit.com/beprepared/ab2mc.html

Practice Exam AB-2

COMPUTER SCIENCE AB
SECTION II

Time — 1 hour and 45 minutes
Number of questions — 4
Percent of total grade — 50

1. Search and Rescue teams need to keep track of the area that has been searched and coordinate their efforts in the field. The area to search will be represented as a class `SearchArea` that has `apmatrix myField` as one of its data members. Each element in `myField` can be a positive integer that represents the number of the team that is currently in that square, -1 if that square has been searched and nothing has been found, or 0 if the square has not been searched. The rows of `myField` are counted from North to South, the columns from West to East. The `SearchArea` class has a constructor that initializes a field of a given size and positions a specified number of teams in their initial locations.

    The teams are initially evenly spaced along the West border (column 0) starting in the NW corner. It is assumed that the number of teams does not exceed the length of the border. The distance between neighboring teams is calculated as:

    $$dist = \left\lfloor \frac{rows}{teams} \right\rfloor$$

    (i.e., number of rows divided by number of teams, <u>truncated</u> to the nearest integer). For example:

Search area with 5 sectors from North to South and 3 sectors from West to East with 2 search teams is declared as follows:	Search area with 7 sectors from North to South and 5 sectors from West to East with 3 search teams is declared as follows:
`SearchArea A(5,3,2);`	`SearchArea A(7,5,3);`
Resulting values in `myField`:	Resulting values in `myField`:

Resulting values in `myField`:

```
            N
       |  0   1   2
     0 |  1   0   0
     1 |  0   0   0
 W   2 |  2   0   0   E
     3 |  0   0   0
     4 |  0   0   0
            S
```

```
            N
       |  0   1   2   3   4
     0 |  1   0   0   0   0
     1 |  0   0   0   0   0
     2 |  2   0   0   0   0
 W   3 |  0   0   0   0   0   E
     4 |  3   0   0   0   0
     5 |  0   0   0   0   0
     6 |  0   0   0   0   0
            S
```

A team is represented by the following structure:

```
struct Team
{
    int row;           // Position in the search area
    int col;
    bool movingEast;   // True if the team is moving East
};
```

In addition to `myField`, the `SearchArea` class includes an `apvector` `myTeams` that keeps track of the teams and their current locations and directions. Note that teams are numbered starting from one while subscripts in `myField` start from 0.

A partial definition of the `SearchArea` class is given below:

```
class SearchArea
{
  public:
    SearchArea(int rows, int cols, int teams); // Constructor
    bool MoveTeam(int teamNum);

    < Other functions not shown >

  private:
    apvector<Team> myTeams;
    apmatrix<int> myField;

    Team NextLocation(int teamNum);
};
```

(a) Write the constructor for the `SearchArea` class, as started below:

```
SearchArea::SearchArea(int rows, int cols, int teams)
  : myField(rows, cols, 0), myTeams(teams)
// precondition:  rows >= teams
// postcondition: myField is initialized with teams evenly
//                spaced along the West border (column 0).
//                myTeams is initialized with coordinates of the
//                teams, all moving East.
```

(b) Write the member function NextLocation as started below. The function returns a Team structure filled with the proposed next location and direction of the team according to the following "team moving algorithm." The team is supposed to move one space in its current direction, East or West, if that move does not take it out of the limits of the field. Otherwise, the team is supposed to move one space South and its previous direction is switched from East to West or from West to East. If the move South also takes the team out of limits, the team is supposed to stay where it is and its direction remains unchanged. The team movements are illustrated below. This function does not actually move a team, just figures out where it should go.

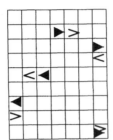

▶ Current location and
    direction of the team

> Proposed next location
    and direction

```
Team SearchArea::NextLocation(int teamNum)
// precondition:  1 <= teamNum <= myTeams.length()
// postcondition: A structure Team is returned. Its
//                members represent the proposed next
//                location and direction of the team, as
//                defined by the team moving algorithm.
```

(c) Write the member function MoveTeam, as started below. You may assume that NextLocation works as specified regardless of what you wrote in Part (b).

```
bool SearchArea::MoveTeam(int teamNum)
// precondition:  1 <= teamNum <= myTeams.length()
// postcondition: The square currently occupied by this
//                team is marked searched and empty.  The
//                next location is calculated according to the
//                team moving algorithm.  If that square has
//                not already been searched and is not occupied
//                by another team, the team is moved to the
//                new location and the function returns true.
//                Otherwise, the team is not moved and the
//                function returns false.
```

2. In a poll of students on their favorite movies, each student chose five of his or her favorites. The results have been stored in a data file in text format. The first line in the file has the number of movie lines to follow. Each subsequent line has the number of votes followed by the movie title. For example, the file may look like this:

```
4
435 Citizen Kane
159 Scream
239 Star Wars
 59 The Enforcer
```

The program that processes this data reads the file into a linked list. A node of the list is represented by the following structure with a constructor:

```
struct MovieVote
{
    int numVotes;
    apstring title;
    MovieVote * next;

    MovieVote (int num, const apstring & t);
};

MovieVote::MovieVote (int num, const apstring & t)
  : numVotes(num), title(t), next(NULL)
{}
```

(a) Write a function that reads the data from a file configured as above and creates a linked list whose nodes contain information from the movie lines of the file, in the same order. For example, the linked list corresponding to the file above will look as follows:

movieList

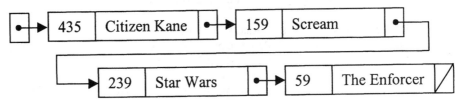

To simplify your code, recall that the getline(istream, apstring &) function provided for the apstring class reads a string from the current position in an input stream until the end of the line and positions the stream at the beginning of the next line. Complete the function Read below.

```
void Read (istream & inFile, MovieVote * & movieList)
// precondition:  inFile is open for reading and the first line
//                contains the count of the movie lines
//                to follow. movieList is NULL, indicating
//                an empty list.
// postcondition: inFile has been read and a node in a
//                linked list has been created for each
//                movie line in the file, preserving the
//                order.  movieList points to the resulting
//                linked list.
```

(b) Complete the function BestMovie below. The function finds the node that corresponds to the movie with the highest score (the first such node if there are ties), removes it from the list, and returns a pointer to that node.

```
MovieVote * BestMovie (MovieVote * & movieList)
// precondition:  movieList is not empty.
// postcondition: The node (or the first of the nodes,
//                if there are ties) that corresponds to
//                the movie with the highest score is removed
//                from movieList.  Returns a pointer to that
//                node.
```

(c)   Write a function that finds the titles of the ten most popular movies in the movie file and places them into an array, ordered from high to low by number of votes. Write the function `FindTopTen` below the following header. You can assume that the functions `Read` and `BestMovie` work as specified regardless of what you wrote in Parts (a) and (b), and that a function `Destroy(MovieVote * movieList)` is provided that properly deallocates all nodes in an unused linked list.

```
void FindTopTen (istream & inFile, apvector<apstring> & top10)
// precondition:  inFile contains at least ten movies;
//                top10.length() == 10
// postcondition: top10 contains the titles of the 10
//                most popular movies in descending order
//                by number of votes.  All temporarily
//                allocated nodes are deleted.
```

3.   This question concerns binary search trees (BSTs) that may contain duplicate values. We assume the following definition: for any node in a BST, all the nodes in its left subtree are less than or equal to the value in the node and all the nodes in its right subtree are greater than or equal to the value in the node. A duplicate of a node may be inserted randomly into the left or the right subtree of that node in order to maintain a more balanced tree.

Out task is to remove all duplicate nodes from the tree. The first step is to learn how we can find and remove duplicates of the root. Note that if the root has a duplicate, it must be the largest node (or one of the nodes with the largest value, if there are several) in the root's left subtree or the smallest node (or one of the nodes with the smallest value) in the root's right subtree. For example:

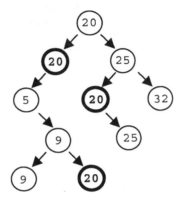

Recall that in a BST, if you start from the root and follow the path going always to the right as far as possible, you will end up in the node that has the largest value. Such a node is always a leaf or has only a left child and therefore it can be easily removed from the tree. Similarly, if you start at the root and go all the way to the left, you will end up in the smallest node. For example:

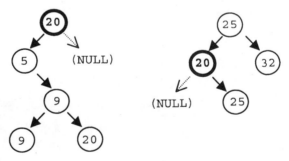

The nodes in a BST will be represented by the following structure:

```
struct TreeNode
{
    int value;
    TreeNode * left;
    TreeNode * right;
};
```

(a) Write a Boolean function `RemoveRightDup` which determines whether the right
subtree of the root has a duplicate of the root and, if so, removes it. The function looks
for the root's duplicate in the leftmost node of the right subtree. It returns true if the
duplicate was found and deleted and false otherwise. The function traces the leftmost
path as far as possible keeping track of the parent of the current node. It then checks
the value in the last node and removes the node if it is a duplicate of the root. To
remove the node, the function attaches its right child to the parent and deletes the node.
Complete `RemoveRightDup` as started below:

```
bool RemoveRightDup (TreeNode * T)
// precondition:  T points to the root of a non-empty BST,
//                possibly with duplicate values.
// postcondition: If a duplicate of the root is found in the
//                leftmost node of the right subtree,
//                that node is removed from the tree and deleted
//                and the function returns true; otherwise
//                returns false.
```

(b) Write a function that eliminates all duplicates from a BST. The tree may have several
or no duplicates for any of its nodes. For example:

Before: After:

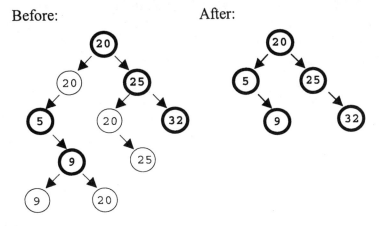

In writing this function you may assume that `RemoveRightDup` works as specified,
regardless of what you wrote in Part (a). Also assume that a function

```
bool RemoveLeftDup (TreeNode * T);
```

is provided. This function is analogous to `RemoveRightDup` of Part (a) but it removes
a duplicate of the root if it is found in the rightmost node of the left subtree. Complete
`EliminateDups` below the following header:

```
void EliminateDups (TreeNode * T)
// precondition:  T points to the root of a non-empty BST.
// postcondition: All duplicates are eliminated from T.
```

4. This question refers to the *Case Study*. It can be found at

    http://www.skylit.com/beprepared/ab2fr.html

A Exam 1

SECTION I: MULTIPLE CHOICE

1. D	11. A	21. C	31. C
2. E	12. A	22. A	32. C
3. A	13. C	23. E	33. A
4. C	14. D	24. B	34. E
5. D	15. E	25. C	35. D
6. C	16. B	26. A	36. E
7. D	17. E	27. D	
8. B	18. B	28. B	
9. E	19. C	29. E	
10. D	20. B	30. E	

Answers to Questions 37-40 can be found at:

http://www.skylit.com/beprepared/a1ans.html

Hints:

3. In II and III, casts into `double` are applied too late.
8. Only g is passed by reference; h remains unchanged.
9. `Smile(1)` prints `smile!` once; `Smile(2) = 2 + Smile(1) = 3` times; `Smile(3) = 3 + Smile(2) = 6` times; `Smile(4) = 4 + Smile(3) = 10` times.
10. `Smile(4), Smile(3), Smile(2), Smile(1), Smile(0) = 5` times
12. h is not an argument or a local variable and it's modified. This is a side effect.
13. `v[i]` initially are all equal to 1.
17. s is const, so `s += space` is an error.
18. I and II divide by zero when `denom` is 0.
20. Odd <u>values</u> not odd subscripts
22. Mystery decrements q by one before returning `(p+q)`.
25. The first three elements become sorted.
26. Subscript is out of bounds for `i = A.length()`.
29. `m[r][c]` are all equal to 1.
31. Binary Search in the customer array in I, Sequential Search in the customer array in II, Binary Search in the array of trips in III.
32. <u>Design 1:</u> $sizeof(name) + 2 \cdot sizeof(int) + n \cdot sizeof(trip)$
    <u>Design 2:</u> $5 \cdot (sizeof(name) + sizeof(trip))$
    If $sizeof(name) = sizeof(trip) = S$, then $S(1 + n) < 10S \Rightarrow 1 + n < 10 \Rightarrow n < 9$
33. `GetTitle` in II and `myInfo` in III are private.
36. If `first = middle = 3` and `last = 4`, the function goes into an infinite loop.

SECTION II: FREE RESPONSE

1.   Part (a)

```
void FillAvgDist(apvector<City> & cityList)
// precondition:  All elements in cityList represent cities.
//                cityList.length() >= 2
// postcondition: The avgDist data element in each city
//                in cityList is set to the average of
//                the distances from that city to all
//                other cities in cityList.
{
    double sum;
    int i, j, len = cityList.length();

    for (i = 0; i < len; i++)
    {
        sum = 0.;
        for (j = 0; j < len; j++)
            if (i != j)
                sum += Distance(cityList[i].location,
                                cityList[j].location);
        // (will work without if (i != j), too)

        cityList[i].avgDist = sum / (len - 1);
    }
}
```

   Part (b)

```
City HubCity(apvector<City> & cityList)
// precondition:  All elements in cityList represent cities.
//                cityList.length() >= 2
// postcondition: The city with the smallest average distance
//                to other cities is found and returned.
{
    int i, h = 0, len = cityList.length();

    FillAvgDist(cityList);

    for (i = 1; i < len; i++)
        if (cityList[i].avgDist < cityList[h].avgDist)
            h = i;

    return cityList[h];
}
```

Part (c)

```
int LongFlight (apvector<City> & cityList,
                         apvector<City> & farCityList)
// precondition:  All elements in cityList represent cities
//                served by an airline.
//                cityList.length() >= 2
//                farCityList.length() >= cityList.length()
// postcondition: The hub city is found and all the cities
//                from cityList whose distance from the hub is
//                greater than (2 * average distance) are copied
//                into farCityList.
//                Returns the number of cities placed into
//                farCityList.
{
    int i, j = 0, len = cityList.length();
    City hub = HubCity(cityList);

    for (i = 0; i < len; i++)
    {
        if (Distance(cityList[i].location,
                    hub.location) > 2. * hub.avgDist)
        {
            farCityList[j] = cityList[i];
            j++;
        }
    }
    return j;
}
```

2.   Part (a)

```
Story::Story (istream & inFile)
   : myCurrWord(0), myCharCount(0), myLineLength(80)
// precondition:  inFile is open for reading.
// postcondition: myCurrWord and myCharCount are initialized
//                to 0, myLineLength is initialized to 80.
//                myWordCount (the number of words in the story)
//                is read from the first line of inFile.
//                apvector myStoryWords is resized accordingly
//                and the story words are read from inFile into
//                myStoryWords.
{
    int i;

    inFile >> myWordCount;
    myStoryWords.resize(myWordCount);

    for (i = 0; i < myWordCount; i++)
        inFile >> myStoryWords[i];
}
```

Part (b)

```
void Story::WriteWord(ostream & outFile)
// precondition:  0 <= myCurrWord < myWordCount;
//                outFile is open for writing.
// postcondition: myStoryWords[myCurrWord], followed by
//                one space character, is written to outFile.
//                If the word and its trailing space do not fit
//                on the current line, it is placed on a new
//                line.  myCharCount is updated appropriately.
//                myCurrWord is incremented by 1.
{
    int n = myStoryWords[myCurrWord].length() + 1;
    if (myCharCount + n > myLineLength)
    {
        outFile << endl;
        myCharCount = 0;
    }
    outFile << myStoryWords[myCurrWord] << ' ';
    myCharCount += n;
    myCurrWord++;
}
```

Part (c)

```
void Story::ReplaceTwoWords(const apstring & word1,
         const apstring & word2, const apstring & word3)
// precondition:  myWordCount >= 2
//                word1, word2, and word3 are different words.
// postcondition: All occurrences of word1 followed by word2
//                are replaced by word3 and myWordCount is
//                decreased accordingly.
{
    int i = 0, j = 0;

    while (i < myWordCount)
    {
        if (i < myWordCount - 1 && myStoryWords[i] == word1 &&
                                   myStoryWords[i+1] == word2)
        {
            myStoryWords[j] = word3;
            i += 2;
        }
        else
        {
            myStoryWords[j] = myStoryWords[i];
            i++;
        }
        j++;
    }
    myWordCount = j;
}
```

3.   Part (a)

```
WordSearch::WordSearch (int rows, int cols)
  : myRows(rows), myCols(cols), myLetters(rows, cols)
// postcondition: myRows and myCols are set to rows and cols
//                respectively, myLetters is resized to
//                rows, cols and filled with random letters.
{
    int r, c;
    for (r = 0; r < myRows; r++)
        for (c = 0; c < myCols; c++)
            myLetters[r][c] = RandomLetter();
}
```

Part (b)

```
bool WordSearch::SearchDown (const apstring & word,
                                      int row, int col) const
// precondition:  0 <= row < myRows and 0 <= col < myCols
//                word has at least one letter and
//                'a' <= word[k] <= 'z' for all letters in word.
// postcondition: Returns true if all letters in word match
//                letters in myLetters, starting at the row, col
//                position and going down with wrap-around to
//                the top row after the bottom row.
{
    int k;

    for (k = 0; k < word.length(); k++)
    {
        if (word[k] != myLetters[row][col])
            return false;
        row++;
        if (row >= myRows) row = 0;
    }
    return true;
}
```

Part (c)

```
bool WordSearch::SearchAll (const apstring & word,
                                    int row, int col) const
// precondition:  0 <= row < myRows and 0 <= col < myCols
//                word has at least one letter and
//                'a' <= word[k] <= 'z' for all letters in word.
// postcondition: Returns true if all letters in word match
//                a string of adjacent letters in myLetters.
//                An element in the matrix may have four
//                (inside), three (on a side), or two (in a
//                corner) adjacent elements.  Self-intersecting
//                strings are allowed.
{
    apstring word1;

    if (word[0] != myLetters[row][col])
        return false;
    else if (word.length() == 1)
        return true;
    else
    {
        word1 = word.substr(1, word.length() - 1);
        return
            (row > 0 && SearchAll(word1, row-1, col)) ||
            (row < myRows - 1 && SearchAll(word1, row+1, col)) ||
            (col > 0 && SearchAll(word1, row, col-1)) ||
            (col < myCols - 1 && SearchAll(word1, row, col+1));
    }
}
```

4.   See

   http://www.skylit.com/beprepared/a1ans.html

A Exam 2

SECTION I: MULTIPLE CHOICE

1. D	11. C	21. B	31. B
2. D	12. C	22. B	32. E
3. B	13. E	23. E	33. E
4. C	14. C	24. B	34. C
5. A	15. B	25. D	35. D
6. C	16. E	26. A	36. D
7. D	17. A	27. C	
8. C	18. B	28. E	
9. B	19. B	29. E	
10. E	20. A	30. D	

Answers to Questions 37-40 can be found at:

http://www.skylit.com/beprepared/a2ans.html

Hints:

6. III displays "many" when m is negative.
10. Because "Computer Science" ends in 'e'
14. In the situation described in (C), <u>Design 2</u> will result in a list that is 10% longer, but each element is only 2/3 the size of the apvector<Date> in <u>Design 1</u>.
15. Binary Search applies
18. If x is not equal to y, then x changes in the first statement. Then (x+y) becomes different in the second statement.
19. $-1 + 2 - 3 + 4 - \ldots + 10 = (-1 + 2) + (-3 + 4) + \ldots + (-9 + 10) = 5$
22. First prints ab, then abx on the same line.
24. The function transposes the upper left n by n corner of the matrix.
25. "Live" would be the value for each element in apvector<CD>, but a CD cannot be constructed with just one string as a parameter.
28. This CD has 13 tracks, and each track has duration 200.
30. Changing one digit or swapping any two digits changes the check digit.
32. Draw does not change the data members of a Rectangle object.

SECTION II: FREE RESPONSE

1. Part (a)

```
double AverageGrade(const APstudent & student)
// precondition:  exams data member in structure student
//                contains a list of all AP exams taken by
//                this student.  The list is not empty and
//                its length is the number of exams taken
//                by student.
// postcondition: Returns the average grade for all
//                AP exams taken by student.
{
    int k, len = student.exams.length();
    int sum = 0;

    for (k = 0; k < len; k++)
        sum += student.exams[k].grade;

    return double(sum) / len;
}
```

Part (b)

```
int Award(const APstudent & student)
// precondition:  exams data member in structure student
//                contains a list of all AP exams taken by
//                this student.  The list is not empty and
//                its length is the number of exams taken
//                by student.
// postcondition: The award level is computed and returned,
//                as follows: 0 for no award, 1 for AP Scholar,
//                and 2 for AP Scholar with Honors.
{
    const int MinGrade = 3;
    int k, len = student.exams.length();
    double years = 0.;
    int aw;

    for (k = 0; k < len; k++)
        if (student.exams[k].grade >= MinGrade)
            years += .5 * student.exams[k].level;
                // Adds 1 for a full-year and .5 for a
                //   half-year subject

    if (years >= 4.0 && AverageGrade(student) >= 3.25)
        aw = 2;
    else if (years >= 3.0)
        aw = 1;
    else
        aw = 0;

    return aw;
}
```

Part (c)

```
void Stats(const apvector<APstudent> & list, int numStudents,
                                apvector<double> & percent)
// precondition:  list contains numStudents students,
//                their exam lists properly filled with data.
// postcondition: percent is resized to hold three elements.
//                percent[0], percent[1], and percent[2] are
//                filled with percentages of all students
//                from the list with no award, AP Scholars,
//                and AP Scholars with Honors, respectively.
{
    apvector<int> count(3, 0);
    int aw;
    int i;

    for (i = 0; i < numStudents; i++)
    {
        aw = Award(list[i]);
        count[aw]++;
    }
    percent.resize(3);
    for (aw = 0; aw <= 2; aw++)
        percent[aw] = 100.0 * double(count[aw]) / numStudents;
}
```

2.   Part (a)

```
bool Remove(apstring & text, const apstring & str)
// precondition:  str is a non-empty string.
// postcondition: If str is found in text, its first occurrence
//                is removed from text and true is returned.
//                Otherwise, text remains unchanged and false
//                is returned.
{
    int pos1, pos2;

    pos1 = text.find(str);
    if (pos1 == npos)
        return false;

    pos2 = pos1 + str.length();
    text = text.substr(0, pos1) +
                text.substr(pos2, text.length() - pos2);

    // Use an example to check your code:
    // text = "0xxx00"; str = "xxx"; text.length() = 6;
    // str.length() = 3
    // pos1 = 1; pos2 = 1+3 = 4;
    // text = text.substr(0, 1) + text.substr(4, 2);

    return true;
}
```

Part (b)

```
apstring RemoveFirstTag(apstring & text)
// precondition:  text is a segment of HTML text which may
//                contain complete HTML tags.  A tag is any
//                substring starting with < and ending with
//                the closest >.
// postcondition: If an HTML tag is found in text, the first tag
//                is removed from text and the tag
//                (including the < and > brackets) is
//                returned.  Otherwise, text remains unchanged
//                and an empty string is returned.
{
    apstring tag;
    int tagpos, taglen;

    tagpos = text.find('<');
    if (tagpos != npos)
    {
        taglen = text.find('>') - tagpos + 1;
        tag = text.substr(tagpos, taglen);
        Remove(text, tag);
        return tag;
    }
    else
        return "";
}
```

Part (c)

```
bool RemoveAllTags(apstring & text)
// precondition:  text is a segment of HTML text which may
//                contain complete HTML tags.
// postcondition: If all HTML tags in text come in matching
//                opening-closing pairs, then all the tags are
//                removed from text and true is returned.
//                (If text has no tags, true is returned.)
//                If tags do not match (i.e., a closing tag
//                comes before the corresponding opening tag
//                or a closing tag is not found),
//                then text remains unchanged and false is
//                returned.
{
    apstring temp = text;
    apstring openTag, closeTag;

    do
    {
        openTag == RemoveFirstTag(temp);
        if (openTag != "")
        {
            if (openTag[1] == '/')
                return false;
            closeTag = "</" +
                    openTag.substr(1, openTag.length() - 1);
            if (!Remove(temp, closeTag))
                return false;
        }
    } while (openTag != "");

    text = temp;
    return true;
}
```

3.   Part (a)

```
Image::Image(istream & inFile)
// precondition:  inFile is a text file in the specified format,
//                open for reading.
// postcondition: The dimensions of the image are read from
//                the first line in inFile and myPixels is
//                resized accordingly.  Pixel data is read
//                from inFile and each element in myPixels
//                is set to 0 for a white pixel and 1 for
//                a black pixel read.
{
    int r, c, rows, cols;
    char ch;

    inFile >> rows >> cols;
    myPixels.resize(rows, cols);

    for (r = 0; r < rows; r++)
        for (c = 0; c < cols; c++)
        {
            inFile >> ch;
            if (ch == 'x')
                myPixels[r][c] = 1;
            else
                myPixels[r][c] = 0;
        }
}
```

Part (b)

```
double Image::FitRatio(const Templ & t, int row, int col) const
// precondition:  row and col define the position
//                of the template -- the upper left corner.
//                The entire template at that position remains
//                within the boundaries of the image.
// postcondition: Returns the fit ratio for the template
//                placed at the (row, col) position.
//                The fit ratio is a weighted sum for all
//                pixels in the image covered by the template,
//                divided by the number of pixels in the
//                template.
{
    int r, c;
    double sum = 0.;

    for (r = 0; r < t.weights.numrows(); r++)
        for (c = 0; c < t.weights.numcols(); c++)
            sum += t.weights[r][c] *
                        myPixels[row + r][col + c];

    return sum / (rows * cols);
}
```

Part (c)

```
char OCR(istream & inFile, const apvector<Templ> & font)
// precondition:  inFile has an image in the specified format
//                and is open for reading.
//                font contains font.length() templates.
// postcondition: Returns a character that corresponds to the
//                best-fitting template from the font or '?'
//                if none of the templates produces a positive
//                fit.
{
    int k;
    int row, col;
    double fit, bestFit = 0.;
    char result = '?';

    Image im(inFile);
    im.LocateChar(row, col);

    for (k = 0; k < font.length(); k++)
    {
        fit = im.FitRatio(font[k], row, col);
        if (fit > bestFit)
        {
            result = font[k].tag;
            bestFit = fit;
        }
    }
    return result;
}
```

4.   See

   http://www.skylit.com/beprepared/a2ans.html

AB Exam 1

SECTION I: MULTIPLE CHOICE

1. D	11. C	21. E	31. D
2. D	12. D	22. E	32. E
3. C	13. A	23. B	33. B
4. B	14. E	24. D	34. B
5. C	15. B	25. C	35. D
6. A	16. C	26. E	36. C
7. D	17. C	27. E	
8. C	18. A	28. A	
9. A	19. C	29. C	
10. D	20. B	30. E	

Answers to Questions 37-40 can be found at:

http://www.skylit.com/beprepared/ab1ans.html

Hints:

1. If x > y and y >= z, then x > z
3. Both a and b refer to num.
4. Quicksort would take at least 9-10 iterations.
8. In Design 2 you can quickly find a given player using Binary Search.
14. If their lengths are the same, two apstrings of digits will compare with the same result as the corresponding numbers.
15. PrintStars Prints stars if list[j] is even, not if j is even.
20. The function never updates myHead, not even when the first node is deleted.
27. In III, Swap A[left] and A[right] ruins the order.
29. When most of the elements fall into one bucket
35. Manipulate makes a mirror image of the tree.

SECTION II: FREE RESPONSE

1.   Part (a)

```
void Screen::ChangeColor(int row, int col)
// precondition:  0 <= row < myNumrows; 0 <= col < myNumcols
// postcondition: The color of the pixel at row, col position
//                is changed from white to black or from black
//                to white.
{
    if (IsBlank(row, col))
        myPixels[row][col] = black;
    else
        myPixels[row][col] = white;
}
```

Part (b)

```
void Magnetize(Screen & S)
// precondition:  S is initialized with black and white pixels.
// postcondition: Each black pixel is moved one space
//                in the same row, column, or diagonally
//                toward the upper right corner.
{
    int r, c;
    int row = 0;
    int col = S.numcols() - 1;

    for (r = row + 1; r < S.numrows(); r++)  // Right col
        if (!S.IsBlank(r, col))
        {
            S.ChangeColor(r, col);
            if (S.IsBlank(r-1, col))
                S.ChangeColor(r-1, col);
        }

    for (c = col - 1; c >= 0; c--)           // Top row
        if (!S.IsBlank(row, c))
        {
            S.ChangeColor(row, c);
            if (S.IsBlank(row, c+1))
                S.ChangeColor(row, c+1);
        }

    for (r = row + 1; r < S.numrows(); r++)  // All the rest
        for (c = col - 1; c >= 0; c--)
            if (!S.IsBlank(r, c))
            {
                S.ChangeColor(r, c);
                if (S.IsBlank(r-1, c+1))
                    S.ChangeColor(r-1, c+1);
            }
}
```

Part (c)

```
Screen operator+ (const Screen & s1, const Screen & s2)
// precondition:  s1 and s2 have the same dimensions.
// postcondition: Returns a new screen that has the same
//                dimensions as s1 and s2.  The new screen has
//                a black pixel in a particular position
//                if and only if either s1 or s2 or both
//                have black pixels in that position.
{
    Screen result(s1.numrows(), s1.numcols());
    int r, c;

    for (r = 0; r < result.numrows(); r++)
        for (c = 0; c < result.numcols(); c++)
            if (!s1.IsBlank(r, c) || !s2.IsBlank(r, c))
                result.ChangeColor(r, c);
    return result;
}
```

2.   Part (a)

```
Node * Unlink (Node * & list)
// precondition:  list points to a non-empty list of nodes.
// postcondition: The first node of list is removed from
//                list, list is updated to point to the next
//                node or NULL.  Returns a pointer to the
//                unlinked node after setting its data member
//                "next" to NULL.
{
    Node * temp = list;
    list = list->next;
    temp->next = NULL;
    return temp;
}
```

Part (b)

```
void Append (Node * & list1, Node * list2)
// precondition:  list1 and/or list2 are either empty (have
//                the value NULL) or point to linked lists.
// postcondition: list2 has been appended at the end of list1.
{
    Node * tail;

    if (list1 == NULL)
        list1 = list2;
    else
    {
        tail = list1;
        while (tail->next != NULL)
            tail = tail->next;
        tail->next = list2;
    }
}
```

Part (c)

```
Node * RadixSort::Gather()
// precondition:  myBins[0], ..., myBins[9] point to lists.
// postcondition: All elements from the lists pointed to
//                by myBins[bin] are gathered into one list.
//                Returns a pointer to the combined list.
//                myBins[0], ..., myBins[9] are left empty.
{
    Node * list = NULL;
    int bin;

    for (bin = 0; bin < 10; bin++)
    {
        Append (list, myBins[bin]);
        myBins[bin] = NULL;
    }
    return list;
}
```

3. Part (a)

```
int Height(TreeNode * T)
// precondition:  T is either NULL or points to
//                a binary tree.
// postcondition: If T is NULL returns -1,
//                otherwise returns the height of
//                the tree pointed to by T.
{
    if (T == NULL)
        return -1;
    return Max(Height(T->left), Height(T->right)) + 1;
}
```

Part (b)

```
void AddSiblings (TreeNode * T, char ch)
// precondition:  T is NULL or points to the root of a
//                binary tree.
// postcondition: Another child with the value ch has been
//                added to each node in T that had exactly
//                one child.
{
    if (T != NULL)
    {
        AddSiblings(T->left, ch);
        AddSiblings(T->right, ch);
        if (T->left == NULL && T->right != NULL)
            T->left = new TreeNode (ch, NULL, NULL);
        else if (T->right == NULL && T->left != NULL)
            T->right = new TreeNode (ch, NULL, NULL);
    }
}
```

Part (c)

```
bool IsFullTree (TreeNode * T)
// precondition:  T points to a non-empty binary tree.
// postcondition: Returns true if T is a full tree,
//                false otherwise.
{
    if (T->left == NULL && T->right == NULL)
        return true;
    else
        return Height(T->left) == Height(T->right) &&
               IsFullTree(T->left) &&
               IsFullTree(T->right);
}
```

4. See

    http://www.skylit.com/beprepared/ab1ans.html

AB Exam 2

SECTION I: MULTIPLE CHOICE

1. D	11. B	21. A	31. E
2. D	12. A	22. C	32. B
3. A	13. C	23. B	33. A
4. C	14. B	24. C	34. D
5. B	15. A	25. A	35. C
6. E	16. E	26. C	36. A
7. D	17. E	27. B	
8. A	18. D	28. D	
9. C	19. E	29. B	
10. A	20. C	30. D	

Answers to Questions 37-40 can be found at:

http://www.skylit.com/beprepared/ab2ans.html

Hints:

1. `m` is passed by value, so it cannot change.
3. `k1` is supposed to be the subscript of the largest element and `k2` — the subscript of the second largest element.
8. `m % 10 == n` tests the units digit in `m`.
9. `count[i]` contains the count of how many times brightness `i` occurs in the image.
12. In (A), precondition for `GetTable` fails.
15. Compares `str[0]` and `str[k]`, not `str[k-1]` and `str[k]`.
17. `Ladder::Ladder(int n, int step)` forgets to resize rungs.
21. Note `push(j)` and `enqueue(j)`, not `push(num)` and `enqueue(num)`
22. See Question 23.
25. Both `p->prev` and `p->next` must be not `NULL`.
26. A complete tree gives the maximum possible number of leaves.
31. Still works fine when `myLength` is 1 and the `while` loop is skipped
34. Insertion Sort works here in $O(n)$ time.
36. Binary Search applies

SECTION II: FREE RESPONSE

1.   Part (a)

```
SearchArea::SearchArea(int rows, int cols, int teams)
  : myField(rows, cols, 0), myTeams(teams)
// precondition:  rows >= teams
// postcondition: myField is initialized with teams evenly
//                spaced along the West border (column 0).
//                myTeams is initialized with coordinates of the
//                teams, all moving East.
{
    int step = rows/teams;
    int k;

    for (k = 0; k < teams; k++)
    {
        myTeams[k].row = k * step;
        myTeams[k].col = 0;
        myTeams[k].movingEast = true;

        myField[k*step][0] = k+1;
    }
}
```

Part (b)

```
Team SearchArea::NextLocation(int teamNum)
// precondition:  1 <= teamNum <= myTeams.length()
// postcondition: A structure Team is returned. Its
//                members represent the proposed next
//                location and direction of the team, as
//                defined by the team moving algorithm.
{
    Team t = myTeams[teamNum-1];

    if (t.movingEast && t.col < myField.numcols() - 1)
        t.col++;
    else if (!t.movingEast && t.col > 0)
        t.col--;
    else if (t.row < myField.numrows() - 1)
    {
        t.row++;
        t.movingEast = !t.movingEast;
    }
    return t;
}
```

Part (c)

```
bool SearchArea::MoveTeam(int teamNum)
// precondition:  1 <= teamNum <= myTeams.length()
// postcondition: The square currently occupied by this
//                team is marked searched and empty.  The
//                next location is calculated according to the
//                team moving algorithm.  If that square has
//                not already been searched and is not occupied
//                by another team, the team is moved to the
//                new location and the function returns true.
//                Otherwise, the team is not moved and the
//                function returns false.
{
     int r = myTeams[teamNum-1].row;
     int c = myTeams[teamNum-1].col;
     Team t;

     myField[r][c] = -1;
     t = NextLocation(teamNum);

     if (myField[t.row][t.col] == 0)
     {
         myField[t.row][t.col] = teamNum;
         myTeams[teamNum - 1] = t;
         return true;
     }
     else
         return false;
}
```

2.   Part (a)

```
void Read (istream & inFile, MovieVote * & movieList)
// precondition:  inFile is open for reading and the first line
//                contains the count of the movie lines
//                to follow. movieList is NULL, indicating
//                an empty list.
// postcondition: inFile has been read and a node in a
//                linked list has been created for each
//                movie line in the file, preserving the
//                order.  movieList points to the resulting
//                linked list.
{
    int n;
    int numVotes;
    char space;
    apstring title;
    MovieVote * p;
    MovieVote * tail = NULL;

    inFile >> n;

    while (n > 0)
    {
        inFile >> numVotes >> space;
        getline(inFile, title);
        p = new MovieVote (numVotes, title);
        if (movieList == NULL)
            movieList = p;
        else
            tail->next = p;
        tail = p;
        n--;
    }
}
```

Part (b)

```
MovieVote * BestMovie (MovieVote * & movieList)
// precondition:  movieList is not empty.
// postcondition: The node (or the first of the nodes,
//                 if there are ties) that corresponds to
//                 the movie with the highest score is removed
//                 from movieList.  Returns a pointer to that
//                 node.
{
    MovieVote * p;
    MovieVote * best = movieList;
    MovieVote * prev = NULL;

    // Find the best movie:
    for (p = movieList->next; p != NULL; p = p->next)
        if (p->numVotes > best->numVotes)
            best = p;

    // Find the previous node:
    p = movieList;
    while (p != best)
    {
        prev = p;
        p = p->next;
    }

    // Unlink best from list:
    if (prev == NULL)
        movieList = best->next;
    else
        prev->next = best->next;

    return best;
}
```

Part (c)

```
    void FindTopTen (istream & inFile, apvector<apstring> & top10)
// precondition:  inFile contains at least ten movies;
//                top10.length() == 10
// postcondition: top10 contains the titles of the 10
//                most popular movies in descending order
//                by number of votes.  All temporarily
//                allocated nodes are deleted.
{
    int k;
    MovieVote * movieList = NULL;
    MovieVote * best;

    Read(inFile, movieList);
    for (k = 0; k < 10; k++)
    {
        best = BestMovie(movieList);
        top10[k] = best->title;
        delete best;
    }
    Destroy(movieList);
}
```

3. Part (a)

```
bool RemoveRightDup (TreeNode * T)
// precondition:  T points to the root of a non-empty BST,
//                possibly with duplicate values.
// postcondition: If a duplicate of the root is found in the
//                leftmost node of the right subtree,
//                that node is removed from the tree and deleted
//                and the function returns true; otherwise
//                returns false.
{
    TreeNode * node = T->right;
    TreeNode * parent = T;

    if (node == NULL)
        return false;

    while (node->left != NULL)
    {
        parent = node;
        node = node->left;
    }

    if (node->value != T->value)
        return false;

    if (parent == T)
        parent->right = node->right;
    else
        parent->left = node->right;

    delete node;
    return true;
}
```

Part (b)

"Postorder" solution:

```
void EliminateDups(TreeNode * T)
// precondition:  T points to the root of a non-empty BST.
// postcondition: All duplicates are eliminated from T.
{
    if (T->left != NULL)
    {
        EliminateDups(T->left);
        // Now at most one duplicate of the root
        //    may remain in the left subtree
        RemoveLeftDup(T);
    }
    if (T->right != NULL)
    {
        EliminateDups(T->right);
        RemoveRightDup(T);
    }
}
```

Less efficient but quite acceptable "preorder" solution:

```
void EliminateDups(TreeNode * T)
// precondition:  T points to the root of a non-empty BST.
// postcondition: All duplicates are eliminated from T.
{
    while (RemoveLeftDup(T));    // The bodies of these while
    while (RemoveRightDup(T));   //    loops are empty

    // Now all duplicates of the root are eliminated
    //    and we can deal with the left and right subtrees:
    if (T->left != NULL)
        EliminateDups(T->left);
    if (T->right != NULL)
        EliminateDups(T->right);
}
```

4. See

http://www.skylit.com/beprepared/ab2ans.html

Index

Notes